THE
PURSUIT
OF
DEATH

HOWARD K. GORDON

ABINGDON • NASHVILLE

THE PURSUIT OF DEATH

Copyright © 1977 by Abingdon

Library of Congress Cataloging in Publication Data

Congdon, Howard K   1941-
  The pursuit of death.

  Bibliography: p.
  Includes index.
  1. Death. I. Title.
BD444.C66   128'.5   76-44308

ISBN 0-687-34915-X

Scripture quotations are from the Revised Standard Version Common Bible, copyrighted © 1973.

Lines on p. 168 from "Do not go gentle into that good night" are from *The Poems of Dylan Thomas*. Copyright 1952 by Dylan Thomas. Reprinted by permission of New Directions Publishing Corporation and of J. M. Dent & Sons Ltd. Publishers and the Trustees for the Copyrights of the late Dylan Thomas.

Lines on p. 168 from "Dirge Without Music," by Edna St. Vincent Millay, are from *Collected Poems,* Harper & Row. Copyright, 1928, 1955, by Edna St. Vincent Millay and Norma Millay Ellis.

MANUFACTURED BY THE PARTHENON PRESS AT NASHVILLE, TENNESSEE, UNITED STATES OF AMERICA

To Jerry,
  in whose absence I reflect upon death;

For Susie and Kristy,
  in whose presence I am grateful for life.

CONTENTS

PREFACE

The true disciple of philosophy . . .
is ever pursuing death . . .

In the year 399 B.C. an old man was preparing himself for death. At the age of 70 he stood condemned by the society he loved, and found himself directly confronting the hour of his execution. He chose to spend his last moments doing exactly what had gotten him into trouble in the first place—discussing philosophy, this time with a handful of friends who braced themselves to face the loss of one for whom they felt only profound admiration and love. The emotional tensions bordered on the unbearable. From time to time several in the group, in an increasingly futile attempt to maintain their composure, were forced to turn away from the man who was to die. Occasionally there were tears shed without shame.

Among that group there was one alone who seemed completely in control of himself—Socrates, the man who was to die. It was Socrates who guided the discussion in the direction of a subject the others would gladly have avoided—a consideration of death. The relaxed manner in which Socrates talked with his friends about death was not a show of bravado. There was no pretense in him. He found in death not only a topic of philosophical fascination, but the very goal of a rational man. Socrates startled his listeners by claiming that "the true disciple of philosophy . . . is ever pursuing death and dying."

The idea that death is something to be pursued sounds somewhat morbid and even suggests a kind of perversion. But Socrates was neither morbid nor perverted. Some translations present Socrates as saying that the "business" of the true philosopher is death and dying, and indeed the term "pursuit" may refer either to a search or to an occupation. Socrates would include both senses. It is the *job* of the true philosopher to search out and explore death.

What is meant by "the true philosopher"? Unfortunately, a philosopher is understood today as one who earns his living doing or teaching philosophy. For Socrates this would amount to a contradiction in terms. He did not believe that one could "teach" philosophy, and therefore it was inappropriate to accept money for being a philosopher. Philosophical knowledge was something to be "uncovered" rather than "acquired." It was already, in some sense, within each and every individual. But until one decided to direct his attention to philosophy such wisdom would lie dormant and utterly useless. Socrates understood a philosopher to be anyone who wished to know himself. "The unexamined life is not worth living," he said. The inference is that life is not worth living unless one is a philosopher. The profession by which one earned his living was irrelevant to Socrates. It was the direction of one's interests which distinguished a philosopher. The true philosopher might be a butcher, a baker, or a candlestick maker. But he strives to understand himself, and ultimately he must consider death.

"The pursuit of death" squares oddly with our inalienable right to "the pursuit of happiness" proclaimed in the Declaration of Independence. Yet the two are not incompatible. Our rights to life, liberty, and the pursuit of happiness may even be grounded in our obligation to pursue death. Jesus said that one who would find his life must lose it. Perhaps this is not so very far removed from Socrates' notion that one who would know himself must necessarily pursue death. The right to a life worth living requires an examination of what it means to die. Both Socrates and Jesus understood that only truth can make us free. The bonds of ignorance carry with them a severe restriction on our choices, our understanding of the options available to us. The unexamined life is not truly free, nor is it really happy. But life cannot be understood apart from a consideration of death.

The pursuit of death, then, is a prime characteristic of anyone who would take seriously his obligation to examine life. Such a pursuit is difficult, for death seems to lie outside the realm of objects which might be examined. It is, in fact, not an "object" in the usual sense at all. It is not something which might be placed on a table or under a microscope. Yet the true disciple of philosophy is driven to understand death. How shall he proceed?

It is the purpose of this book to pursue death, to suggest ways in which this might be done, and to speculate upon the possible outcome of such efforts. Inevitably we shall discover that we have raised more questions than we have answered, if indeed we are able to answer any questions at all. But the example of Socrates cannot be ignored. We, like him, confront the hour of our death. Let us spend some of our remaining moments pursuing death.

INTRODUCTION

It was the first funeral I had ever been to—and it was mine. It was not, of course, my death. But it was my funeral. I had the unhappy responsibility of conducting the service for the burial of an eleven-year-old boy. I had never thought much about death, about its meaning or the theologies and rituals that go with it. I knew, however, that my avoidance of these considerations had been a serious mistake. I had accepted my first pastoral responsibilities in what was to be a brief but intense career as a minister. I took the job hoping desperately that nobody would die. Of course it had to happen, but my fervent desire was that these people would be gracious enough to allow me to avoid coming to grips with the fact of death at least until I was "ready" to deal with it. I was not ready. There were too many questions I had not even begun to consider, let alone answer. Why do we die? The question was asked by the mother of the boy I was burying. It was a tense moment, one I will never forget. So distraught had she become over the loss of her son that she jumped into the grave in order to embrace the coffin. The only coherent words she could utter were directed at me as she was being helped from the grave: "Why, why?" I felt hopelessly inadequate. It would not do, obviously, to answer "heart attack." That was the medical answer to the question, but it was not a medical answer she sought. I was unwilling even to attempt a theological answer, and the metaphysics of the event totally escaped me. Why must we die?

Not long after my initial trial by fire, I was actually to witness a person die. This time it was an elderly woman who had suffered extensively. Although everyone said that it was a blessing, the moment was no less intense. Something very significant had happened, an event marking perhaps the most important moment of a person's existence. She was alive one minute earlier, and now she was dead. Everything was still there. Nothing physical seemed to be missing. The cells of the body, the various organs were still there. A detailed photograph of the woman just prior to her death would have been indistinguishable from a photograph of her now. Nothing was missing—but that was absurd. "She" was missing. Where did she go? What had happened? What *is* death?

It is one thing to deal with those who remain and to try and transcend the loss of a loved one yourself. It is another area entirely when one attempts to understand just what death is and to discover the implications of personal extinction. I had been adequately trained in the psychology of death insofar as my obligations to the living were concerned. There is an increasing body of literature dealing with the psychological aspects of death, and this is an important area of study which deserves extensive attention. But my questions were not psychological. People often wonder what to say to those who are left. But there is no need to be profound. The silent expression of sympathy in one's presence is more important than eloquence. I could handle that. My confusion was philosophical. Death simply made no sense to me. I could not understand what death was or what it meant. I had no training in the metaphysics of death. In my efforts to pursue an understanding of death I have organized seminars entitled "Philosophy of Death," a not so very clever way of being paid for studying what I was interested in anyway. The response has been startling. It would seem that I am not the only one with such an interest. In addition, it became clear that, while there is a good deal of writing currently available on the topic of death, there are few books dealing with death as a philosophical puzzle. The questions which most concern me are not resolved in the analysis of death as a psychological problem. A major portion of my curiosity is frankly academic in nature, and I find little help in the study of social attitudes, funeral customs, and the like. There is no denying the importance of these areas, but my interests lie elsewhere. Death presents itself to me as an enigma, an intriguing mystery defying analysis, yet taunting in its significance. Can something so ultimately significant also be ultimately inscrutable? We must try and find out.

Our purpose, then, will be to pursue death both as a metaphysical and an existential event. We cannot entirely be objective in our consideration of death. We will not pretend that death can be approached simply as an event "out there" in the world having no importance for us as subjective beings. Death is, in part, an objective metaphysical reality. It raises questions not easily answered within the confines of the laboratory. But death is also a subjective existential reality. It comes to us not simply as one more area of inquiry, but as an ultimate personal threat. We are more than academically involved in the study of death. We are participating in the very process of death. Unless we can view death as a metaphysical event which touches us at our very deepest level, we will necessarily fail to grasp its full import.

In pursuing death as a metaphysical event we are taking on a formidable task. It is not easy to gain understanding in the metaphysics of anything. The term "metaphysics" is one of the fuzziest in philosophy, itself one of the fuzzier disciplines around. The Greek roots of the word "metaphysics" suggest an area of exploration which literally goes beyond *(meta)* the realm of physics *(physika)*. But that does not tell us very much. What does it mean to pursue death beyond its physical manifestations? The assumption here is that there is much more to death than is revealed at the level of physics. Death can properly be studied as a biological event. It does put in an appearance at the physical level. But in spite of the fairly thorough biological knowledge we have of death, it is quite obvious that death remains a very dark mystery. If we grant that we possess a basic understanding of death as a physical or medical event, and if we still sense that there is a genuine mystery, an ultimate ignorance, in our understanding of death, this suggests that it is at the level of metaphysics that death is not understood. If we assume that death is simply the irreparable breakdown in the biological functioning of the body, then there really is no mystery. If death is nothing more than its physical manifestations, then we already understand death, at least in a basic sense. But no one seriously believes that there is no real mystery about death. The fact is that death is a real puzzle. There can be, for example, no question about our prospects for immortality if we view death as a strictly biological event. If death is fully explained and understood at the level of physics, then immortality is obviously an illusion. If death is an event which comes to the body and if, further, we ourselves are nothing more than those bodies which die, then belief in immortality must be quite irrational unless we develop a cogent argument for the resurrection of the body. Yet many otherwise rational people wonder. Perhaps immortality is an illusion. But the fact is that we just do not know that. If there is a mystery about death, it would seem that it must be at the level of metaphysics. When we ask whether consciousness survives death, we are probing past the limits of physics. When we inquire into the nature of ultimate reality and our relationship to it we are exploring realms beyond physics. We are into metaphysics.

Metaphysics is an area which has a transcendent quality about it. It seems to be a region which lies beyond the known, and must therefore remain unknown. But we should never assume that the parameters of what can be known are defined by the physicist. We are made for speculation beyond those regions in which we can have certainty, into realms which admit only of degrees of probability. We are multidimensional creatures, with hungers which cannot be satisfied in any single dimension. If we enter areas of speculation in which angels fear to tread, it is only because we are what we are. Should we deny ourselves the pleasures of metaphysics, we will negate an aspect of ourselves which seems to separate us from the beast. But we cannot be careless. Metaphysical speculation invites a certain kind of sloppiness. Many blatantly irrational and unsupported theories parade about under the cloak of metaphysics. The assumption seems to be that if we can transcend physics, then we can transcend logic and intellectual honesty. That assumption will not be made in this book. Of course there are legitimate questions which go beyond the data of physics. But to the extent that we deny those data, or oppose the rigorous structure of logic, we degrade ourselves and lose our status as seekers after the truth. Philosophers are said to be lovers of wisdom. We can do no better in our exploration of death than to pursue the truth as philosophers.

The subject, then, demands intellectual honesty. But it demands more. It requires the more difficult quality of psychological honesty. In probing the mysteries of death we are probing into the very bowels of our being. We are dying. The significance of death is not in its quality as an event that comes to all people. "All men are mortal." The phrase is so innocuous as to be nearly empty of content. It is used, not in the study of man as a mortal being, but as the paradigm of a major premise in the study of syllogistic logic. It is not the mortal status of all men that particularly affects me. It is my own inevitable doom. Certainly something would be lost in the story told by Jesus of the man who devoted all his attention to building bigger barns for his crops if this element of death were ignored. Having decided upon his course of action, the man became content with himself, thinking that he had achieved the security all men seek. "But God said to him, 'Fool! This night your soul is required of you; and the things you have prepared, whose will they be?'" (Luke 12:20). The stunning power of that verse would be completely lost had it read, "Fool! All men are mortal." It is the stark, inescapable fact of our *own* death that causes us to wince, not the mortal quality of mankind.

It is clearly impossible to deal adequately with every facet of death within the confines of a single book—or perhaps even a library of books. Some of the ramifications of death will of necessity be ignored, not simply because of the limitations inherent in any book, but also because many of them are unknown or not well understood. But what are the options? Is there any reason to assume that nothing can be learned about death apart from the medical aspects of the event? Are we required to suppose that death must forever remain a mystery, that any attempt to progress in our understanding of death will necessarily be frustrated? The fact that many people make these assumptions is hardly conclusive. The topic is an important one. Hardly anyone would deny that. Our choices, then, are basically two: either we will make some, perhaps faltering and inadequate, attempts to understand death or we will not. The issue is simply too significant, too exciting, for us to choose to ignore it. We may fail, in which case we will be no worse off than we are now. But we may just begin to succeed.

CHAPTER 1
Some Problems

In a California university a philosophy professor lies in a coffin while his students conduct his funeral. He is not dead. It is his way of bringing the reality of death to his students in as vivid a way as possible (short of his own death). A Cleveland man announces the invention of his Eternal Monument, a device which combines the services of a tombstone, a tape player, and a television set. Powered by solar energy, it features organ music and movies of the deceased. A Nashville firm promotes the nation's first high-rise mausoleum as an opportunity for the average citizen to enjoy the "preferred burial . . . of kings, queens, and presidents," counting, apparently, on some sort of innate desire for aboveground crypts in the manner of the Egyptian tombs. Not to be outdone, an Atlanta mortician features drive-in viewing, which allows one to pay last respects without leaving the comforts of one's air-conditioned car. After all, it can get very warm in Atlanta. In New York City a doctor freely admits injecting air into a patient's veins in order to kill him and is acquitted by a jury. A made-for-television movie quickly adopts this motif for network entertainment. In another part of Fun City, Columbia University's Foundation of Thanatology sponsors a well-attended conference on death. On a less spectacular level, a number of hospitals are beginning to train "thanotherapists," who can specialize in meeting the needs of dying patients. Sensitivity sessions are raising individual consciousness to an awareness of death as inevitable, personal, and highly significant. Several colleges and universities are offering seminars dealing with death. They are quickly filled, and many are turned away. A local high school even offers a mini-course on death. A famous columnist, having learned that he has but a short time to live because of an incurable disease, decides to devote his remaining time to writing about his experience of impending death. Scenes like these, ranging from the bizarre to the profound, indicate that a thoughtful, serious confrontation with the concept of death is an idea whose time has come.

The reasons for this activity are not easily determined. One might wonder just why it is that we find today an apparent growing interest in the subject of death. It might be maintained that this is really nothing new. Early Greek and Roman philosophy spent much of its energy attempting to provide a rational account of death. Democritus and Epicurus, four centuries prior to the birth of Christ, presented a theory of death giving a materialistic interpretation of the fate of the soul. In a surprisingly sophisticated way they argued that, because reality was atomic in nature, whatever was real was composed of atoms. This would include the soul. At death, then, the soul, like the body, disintegrates and survives only as scattered atoms no longer capable of sensation. They and their disciples concluded on the basis of this analysis that fear of death was one of the most irrational of emotions. Their understanding of death indicated that it was a status absolutely devoid of experiential content. Since it cannot be experienced it cannot hurt, and therefore should not bother us. Further, since death entails the extinction of awareness, the fear of death is literally equivalent to being afraid of nothing. And that does sound a bit irrational. These sentiments were later echoed by Lucretius, a Roman poet and philosopher who accepted the analysis of the atomists.

Socrates, of course, dealt extensively with death, believing that the goal of the philosopher is death. His martyrdom remains even today the paradigm of how to die. Plato presents Socrates as advancing several arguments for the immortality of the soul. These were later accepted by Plotinus, and so it goes. The history of philosophy is in part the history of man's pursuit of death. The tradition is carried on today by the Existentialists, who give evidence of a deep concern for the implications of death. There is something to the belief that the contemporary interest in death is really nothing new.

Except that it *is* new. We are not witnessing simply a philosophical concern with death. This new interest is much wider. Something is different, and it would be difficult to argue seriously that the mood of the times has not changed. It can be argued that the interest in death is due to a relatively recent loss of absolutes. It is the natural result of the death-of-God phenomenon. With the absence of the idols of our tribe which once comforted us and provided an ultimate security, we cannot be surprised that man has begun to consider the implications of his loss. What does the eclipse of God mean to me when I die? The rather thorough questioning of moral and theological absolutes, which is a relatively recent event, might easily begin to turn our culture toward an examination of its destiny. It might well create within an individual the desire to ponder what it all means to him.

Or maybe it is all a part of a larger crumbling of the foundations. Perhaps the contemporary interest in death is precisely the morbid fascination one might expect from a civilization in its period of decay. The loss of hope is symbolized by death. Our concern for death may simply be a reflection of a cultural pessimism.

Or perhaps we have grown up. It may be that civilization is suffering not from the slings and arrows of senility, but rather from the growing pains of adolescence. We may have arrived at a stage in which we are ready to deal with the very serious issue of our own death. It has been noted by others that the topic of death today has certain similarities to the status occupied by sex at an earlier time. As long as the analogy is not pressed too far, such a comparison is quite valid. A serious study of sex was at one time very nearly impossible and even today can be difficult. The psychological threat of sex is expressed in the various taboos which cling to it as a legitimate area of study, in the tendency of some to giggle or look at their feet whenever the topic is raised, in the apparent inability of others to talk about sex except as a joke, and so on. Sex is threatening in proportion to its power and importance, and perhaps its mystery. Even today, in what many believe to be a relatively open and permissive society, a serious discussion of sex is a tricky affair. But the situation has changed. With the growing acceptance of sex as an important aspect of our lives and therefore deserving of careful study we now know much more about its physiological and psychological aspects than we once did. Something similar may be happening with respect to death. The very threat of death is at least in part a function of our ignorance about it. Such ignorance is neither accidental nor necessary. It is a product of deliberate design. We have carefully cultivated an ignorance of death by draping it with various social taboos, thereby discouraging exploration of the topic. Many people cannot bring themselves to speak directly about death and are reduced to less threatening euphemisms of the dead as having "passed away," or "fallen asleep," or "gone on to a greater glory," or whatever. We even speak of old people who most directly confront the grave as "senior citizens" enjoying their "golden years." Under other circumstances such phrases would be considered rather mawkish. But language is our most important tool, and it can be used to help us avoid ourselves when that is what we want. The fact is that death, like sex, is too basic and too important to us as human beings to be hidden forever. It must eventually be faced as directly and as honestly as possible. And that is just what is happening. Just as sex was dragged out from behind the barn, death is being stripped of its secrecy. It has to happen. We cannot be served by ignorance.

Philosophy would appear to be especially well suited to probe the mysteries of death. It was, after all, the death of Socrates that tore Plato loose from his aristocratic ties and set the stage for subsequent philosophical speculation about the nature of the soul and the proper attitude toward death. The mystery of death is more metaphysical than biological. The real questions lie on the other side of the microscope. Philosophy, perhaps more than any other discipline, has the proper credentials for exploring such regions. Philosophy, in spite of the efforts of certain linguistic analysts, is at its heart metaphysics. It provides for legitimate speculation beyond the laboratory data. If a soul cannot be microscopically dissected, it can be conceptually analyzed. If purpose and meaning and value are not to be found via a computer print-out, they can be subjected to the rigors of philosophical analysis. And these are, after all, the mysteries of death. If they are to be resolved, we must pursue a philosophy of death.

It is not an easy task. The consideration of death presents many difficulties, some of which are encountered nowhere else. There is first of all a natural reluctance to think about one's own extinction. Death carries with it the most serious of all threats, paradoxically expressed by Heidegger as "the possibility of the impossibility of existence." It implies the final, inevitable victory of nothingness over the only thing we really have—our being. And it is not easy to wrestle with our own doom.

But there are other, perhaps more serious, difficulties in any consideration of death. There are conceptual difficulties involved in the study of death. It is first of all psychologically, if not logically, odd to conceive of our own death. If death is literally our very extinction, involving a complete loss of awareness, how are we to think of it? How can we in any way imagine what death is like if death entails the inability to imagine at all? It is at least puzzling to try and get a handle on the very concept of nothingness and apparently impossible to conceive of our own negation. Since conception involves awareness it is not at all clear just how we are to understand our eventual state of non-awareness. Such a task, involving the attempt to increase our knowledge of something which, by its very nature must reside outside the boundaries of our earthly experience, seems logically hopeless. How can we possibly expect to know the unknowable, or become aware of what it means to lose awareness itself? It is like trying to think specifically of absolutely nothing at all.

It is, of course, too early to let such a formidable obstacle turn us aside. After all, this is only the first chapter. It may be that death really cannot be studied because of this conceptual difficulty. But it is not necessary to succumb to such a first-round knockout. There is ample precedent for us to pursue a study of what appears to be intrinsically beyond our ken. Freud, after all, did not hesitate to tell us about the unconscious mind. The unconscious is, by definition, forever removed from our awareness. Whatever we can realize about it must be a conscious realization and therefore at best we can have only inferential knowledge of whatever levels of consciousness may exist on the other side of awareness. We cannot, for example, become aware of subconscious drives and motivations unless and until they poke themselves into our conscious minds, but then they are no longer subconscious. But this hardly slows the Freudian analyst down. And it does appear that we can make some respectable guesses about the dynamics of subconscious processes. At any rate, we do. Further, many philosophers have believed that, because we are forever necessarily restricted to our own subjective experiences of the world, it is therefore impossible to know objective reality directly. And there is an obvious sense in which this is certainly the case. When looking at a carrot, for example (it could be anything—even a squash), we do not really experience, or even see, the carrot itself. We experience, or see, what some philosophers have referred to as sense-data, some informational sort of stuff somehow thrown back at us by the objects "out there." But we never see those objects. We see (or smell or hear or taste or touch) the sense-data, or what Kant called the phenomena, and we gratuitously assume that they bear some sort of worthy relationship to the mysterious noumena which (we suppose) produce them.

This is why philosophers occasionally toy with the idea of solipsism—the view that the individual (in my case, me) is the only reality, the whole of existence. It is a view which requires a major effort to take seriously, but one which is notoriously difficult to disprove. After all, what do you know about the world other than your own subjective ideas of it? We cannot be sure that our idea of a carrot bears any resemblance at all to the vegetable itself, and we seem able to make a decent salad in spite of our inability to experience the objective carrot.

It would be a bit quirky to say that death is like a carrot, but it is not too much to point out that our apparent inability to experience death directly should not deter us from attempting to learn more about it. Just as we can make a passable salad with vegetables we can never hope to know firsthand, perhaps we can begin to toss an acceptable philosophical salad from metaphysical vegetables which elude our direct grasp. Furthermore, there is an aspect of death which is not so elusive—dying. There is an important distinction to be made between death and dying. Dying is a process. It is a series of events occurring within the parameters of life. We can experience dying, even if we cannot experience death. Dying is a process we can experience and

22

therefore study directly. Death is an event somehow outside our everyday experience which must be approached in other ways. Dying, unlike death, can be experienced in many ways. The shape of dying is protean. It comes in many forms. We sometimes can have an influence on the quality of dying, although many of its aspects are normally beyond our control.

Broadly speaking, dying must fall into one of two categories. Either we are aware of our impending death as an imminent event or we are not. I once watched a man dying for a little over a year. He had been told that he had at most one year to live, and he beat that estimate by only a few days. He was aware of his dying. Toward the end he was even able to describe quite vividly the feeling of his approaching death. The effects of this knowledge on his character were profound. He was able to take advantage of this experience and use it to gain some startling personal insights. I watched him as he was transformed from a man whose daily concern reached no further than the can of beer which was always within arm's length, to one whose interests led him to lengthy and significant assessments of what it meant to be alive and what it meant to die. Such an experience is denied to most people. Death too often takes us by surprise, robbing us of any opportunity to acquire a larger perspective of ourselves and reality. One who dies unexpectedly in his sleep or from a heart attack is often envied. "That's the way I want to go—quickly and painlessly." Such sentiments are common. But they may not be as reasonable as they sound. We are, in a sense, always dying, but it is not generally the case that we are brought starkly face to face with the reality of our own death. Because death is a part of our very definition it would seem reasonable to suppose that we can learn more about ourselves from a consideration of death. But most of us never make the effort unless we ourselves are threatened by imminent death and are aware of that threat. There is a sense in which we are genuinely cheated if death should catch us unawares. This is a consideration physicians would do well to ponder as they make a decision whether or not to tell a patient that he has a terminal disease. It is probably true that some patients should not be told that they are going to die. Others definitely should be told, not simply on the basis that they can take it, but more importantly because they can use it.

Within the categories of awareness or non-awareness, dying can be either slow or rapid. The difference can be very important. Knowledge of one's impending death generally produces a series of fairly well-defined stages in the psyche. But this is a process which takes time. The man who was aware of his inevitable death for an entire year was able to work his way through each of these levels to achieve the insights that finally came to him. A woman I knew was not so fortunate. She had dabbled in faith-healing, hoping to be able to effect a cure for what she called "the mopes," a constant feeling of listlessness often accompanied by pain. She was rushed to the emergency room only after she had finally collapsed into unconsciousness. Exploratory surgery revealed cancer at such an advanced stage that there was simply nothing which could be done. She was told that she probably had less than a month to live. In fact it was exactly three weeks. Her dying was too quick. It was impossible to digest. There was not enough time for her to work through the implications of her situation, and her dying was fraught with mental as well as physical agony. She left a bewildered husband and six anguished children. There are clearly important differences in the qualities associated with slow and rapid dying.

Another important quality of dying has to do with whether it is painful or not. I once watched a man dying of cancer of the sinuses. I had not known that there even was such a horrible form of cancer. His pain had gone beyond the ability of any drugs to alleviate. Because his suffering was so intense he was quite unable to direct his attention to anything else. It was not a good dying. Being relatively free from pain is important not only in terms of physical comfort, but also because pain can be so demanding of our mental energies. It can block our understanding of what is happening to us.

Of course there are other forms of dying which deserve consideration. Suicide, euthanasia, and capital punishment come to mind. There are distinctions to be made in the source of our dying, whether from disease, by accident, by our own hand, or by the will of others. But what it all comes down to is that dying can be ennobling or humiliating. It is not really odd to speak of a noble dying. Dying can sometimes bring out the most admirable qualities of a person. One can imagine dying bravely or for a worthy cause. It is not at all unusual for people to grow intensely fond of one who is dying, not simply out of sympathy, but for genuinely worthy reasons. Individuals can in fact grow up during the process of dying. They can, and often do, exhibit qualities previously unsuspected in them. Our admiration for a dying person can be based on very legitimate reasons. And our sadness can be increased as we recognize the tragedy of losing an individual of genuine worth.

There are indeed many ways of dying. There is presumably only one form of death. Dying is an important process. Because it occurs while we are yet alive it can be studied. We can use it or abuse it. But at least we can begin to understand it. We can think of dying. But it is not clear how we can think of being dead. The process of dying ends at the moment of death. The individual is then no longer dying; he is dead. An understanding of the process of dying is at least possible because we may expect to experience it. But the most intractable problems in any philosophy of death have to do not with the process of dying, but with being dead. And how can we hope to experience being dead? At this point we are at the heart of the mysteries of death.

25

Somehow we are squeezed from reality as we know it into a dimension so alien to us that nothing in our philosophical bag of tricks seems adequate to the task of understanding just what has happened. How are we to analyze our death if it involves our very extinction? Of what possible use can philosophical speculation be in an area which by its very definition excludes not simply the only experience we know, but perhaps experience itself? It is a formidable problem.

The problem is not resolved even with the assumption that some sort of nonphysical awareness is possible after death. The various theoretical notions of life after death all encounter the difficulty of expressing just what is meant by an experience apart from the body. What kind of experience is possible, or even conceivable, without the physical senses? Without the ability to see or hear or taste or smell or touch, what could possibly be left? Even acknowledging that something might remain, how can we know about it? How can it be explored? It would seem that we must somehow penetrate that ultimate barrier between the living and the dead if we are to develop an adequate conceptual framework for our theories about death. The fact is that we are viewing the issue from the wrong side. We are attempting to understand what is on the other side of a curtain without being allowed even to peek at it. It appears that we are reduced to philosophical guessing games.

These difficulties generate still another problem of special interest to philosophy. There is a philosophical troll living under our metaphysical bridges, threatening to prevent our ever crossing the boundaries of empirical data. The troll is known as "The Verification Principle." He demands a price for every metaphysical speculation, insisting, not unreasonably, that all meaningful propositions have a cash value. That is, they must commit themselves to one set of circumstances to the exclusion of some other set. Further, it must be possible to delineate some events or situations such that, were they to occur, the proposition would clearly be established as being true or false. In other words, all meaningful statements must take a chance. They must, at least in theory, be verifiable or falsifiable. Should they prove to be compatible with any and all conceivable events, that can only mean that they have not really said anything. Thus, for example, while I might bravely assert that "the theory of gravity is heavier than lead," the philosophical troll demands his price. What is the meaning of such an assertion—i.e., what specifically does it proclaim? What does it deny? Under what circumstances might it be proved, or shown to be false? I would not be allowed to cross his bridge. Would I be any better off in presenting certain speculations about my own existential status after death? Perhaps, but I must be clear in specifying just how such propositions might be verified or falsified before the troll will let me pass. And that could prove to be a genuine problem.

The pursuit of death, then, encounters a number of serious obstacles. Some of these have been mentioned and, of course, there are others. The evidence indicates that we are at last arriving at a period in our development as a culture when it is not only legitimate to probe the mysteries of the grave, it is demanded. We need not particularly trouble ourselves with the respectability of such a study. The widespread concern with the various aspects of death suggests that we have outgrown a certain metaphysical adolescence during which we were unable to bring ourselves to sit down and reason about our own death. The topic is beginning to assault us from all sides. The fact that you are reading this book indicates some willingness on your part to overcome whatever resistance you may feel toward dealing with death. The taboos, while not completely banished, have been weakened. That you are willing to attack the ultimate metaphysical puzzle does not mean we can ignore some very real fears which may remain. The demons of fear need not be entirely exorcised before we can confront our destiny. But they must be subdued. They must be under our control or we may be making a serious mistake. A once popular cigarette now brags that "they're not for everybody." Philosophy of death is not for everybody. It is a serious business to probe the dark areas of death. Those who have recently suffered the loss of someone close, who are deeply involved in the process of dying, or who have marginal control over those suicidal impulses which occasionally come to everyone have some homework to do before confronting the specter of death.

But let us assume that we are psychologically prepared. The topic is recognized as an important one that deserves our attention. There is no longer any need to violate radically any of the social taboos in our consideration of death. It is an accepted area of intellectual study. The reluctance of the psyche to examine its own destiny is the very least of our problems. Having resolved these initial difficulties, we may confidently say that we are ready. We are willing. Our task now is to determine whether we are able. It remains an open question whether it is possible to study our own death in any logically satisfactory way. We do not yet know just what avenues are available to us when it comes to a verification of whatever theories we might develop or discover. The psychological problems involved are at least in part resolved merely by our willingness to approach the issue. We cannot tell whether the other difficulties can be overcome until we are well into our subject matter.

CHAPTER 2
Toward a Definition of Death

We are not off to a good start. One of the most serious problems in the study of death was not even mentioned in the previous chapter. We really are not sure how to define death. In one sense the pursuit of death is nothing more than the pursuit of a definition. We cannot understand death until we know what it is. But knowing what it is would appear to be another way of saying that we understand it. How, then, do we begin to resolve our ignorance about death? It is an old question, not at all unique to the topic of death. But it is a legitimate one. Do we create an arbitrary definition of death, *ex nihilo,* and work from there? Or are we reduced to striking out blindly in all directions at once, hoping to stumble somehow into the knowledge we seek? At this point we could easily devote the rest of the book to the problems of epistemology, trying to figure out just how it is that we seem able to pursue knowledge in areas in which we are ignorant. Either we know what we are after or we do not. If we do, there is no point in wasting our time attempting to gain what we already have. If we do not, how will we recognize it when we find it? But the problems of how we learn are not really our concern here. Somehow it is done. Our task now is to do it, and it would seem that our first efforts ought to be devoted to the development of a working definition of death—being careful to see that the definition does not settle prematurely the major issues involved in the study of death. It is likely that such a definition of death at this early stage of our exploration will be expanded, modified, or even abandoned later on. But we must have some basic idea of just what it is that we are struggling with.

And it would seem that we do. Perhaps death is like pornography[1] and our knowledge of what it is is analogous to that of the Supreme Court justice who declared, with respect to pornography, "I don't know what it is, but I know it when I see it." Perhaps death is a sort of metaphysical pornography—an event utterly without redeeming social value, possibly even to the extent of appealing to our prurient interests. But surely we can do better.

Although our main concern is not with the medical or physical aspects of death, we cannot reasonably deny that death is very much a physical event. There are some who would insist that death is *only* a physical event. In any case, we might do well to begin here. To the extent that death is a physical event we can expect to find some assistance in defining it from the medical profession. After all, it is the physician whose job it is to help us postpone the dreaded event. He should, therefore, be in a position to identify just what it is that he is fighting. But alas, some of the vaunted oracles of the noble profession of medicine have a Delphic quality about them. The fact is that a satisfactory medical definition of death is still being worked out, with more than one suggestion that the attempt to define death precisely will never succeed.

The history of medicine is, of course, dotted with examples of persons who, having been pronounced dead, literally sat up to announce their disagreement with the verdict. J. J. Bruhier-d'Ablaincourt, a French physician in the mid-eighteenth century, documented numerous instances of premature burial and certificates of death which subsequently had to be torn up on the basis of obviously irrefutable evidence.[2] His solution to such embarrassments was to advocate deferring burial until after the onset of the early stages of putrefaction. His suggestion is of no help to us, however. There is general agreement that death has certainly occurred sometime prior to that state, and in any case we cannot seriously define death as the rotting of flesh, accompanied by an obnoxious odor. There are too many diseases of the living which would fit such a definition. Nor are the difficulties of determining the moment of death limited to the remote history of medicine. Even today there are occasional errors in the attempt to determine the moment of death. In war, for example, mistakes of this sort, while unusual, are not unknown. There are reports from time to time of men being pronounced dead on the battlefield after failing to respond to resuscitation efforts, who eventually make complete recoveries.

Most examples of an incorrect diagnosis of death are due more to carelessness than to ignorance. During periods of war or other emergency a determination of death is often based upon a cursory examination of the body by the harried physician or sometimes the judgment of nonmedical personnel. It is probable that such cases would be extremely rare indeed if all pronouncements of death were the result of intensive and conscientious examination of the body by a qualified authority. But there would still be some mistakes simply because we are not exactly sure just what we are looking for. The traditional indicators of death focused on the absence of respiration and heartbeat, the drying of the corneas and subsequent flaccidity of the eyeballs, insensitivity to electrical and physical stimuli, a pallid complexion, relaxation of the sphincter muscles, and of course rigor mortis. These are still cited as genuine signs of death. A good deal of consideration is being given today to the electroencephalogram (EEG), a device which measures the electrical impulses of the brain. A flat EEG (no bumps in the lines on the graph) would indicate a dead—or at least an inactive—brain. Because many portions of the brain are extremely vulnerable to any loss of oxygen, even for a few seconds, it has been suggested that death be defined as an absence of any brain activity (as indicated by a flat EEG) for a period of, say, five minutes. Under normal circumstances, this would appear to be a reasonable position. But "normal circumstances" take their definition in opposition to abnormal ones. A London physician has reportedly cited two cases in which patients who exhibited flat EEGs for several hours subsequently made a complete recovery.[3] They had been victims of severe barbiturate poisoning. Similar examples have been reported in the United States. Perhaps the presence of certain drugs can be a significant alteration in what otherwise would be normal circumstances. Experiments with freezing techniques to produce a state of suspended animation indicate that a drop in temperature can lead to similar results. Dr. Henry K. Beecher of the Harvard medical school has warned against complete reliance on the EEG in determining death. He specifically excludes from this procedure "individuals who are under central nervous system depressants, or whose internal temperature is below 96 degrees Fahrenheit."[4] Further complicating matters is the knowledge that a number of diseases can produce trance states distinguishable from death only with considerable difficulty. It simply will not do to depend on a mirror held under the nose.

It should be noted that it is of more than academic interest that we develop an accurate definition of death which will allow us to determine the moment at which death has occurred. A murder trial in California was recently jolted when the defense made a case resting entirely upon the difficulties of defining death. The accused had shot a man (the prosecution said "murdered"). The victim was pronounced dead, and his still beating heart was removed and transplanted into another patient. The defense attorneys insisted that, as the heart was still functioning when it was removed, their client could not be guilty of murder. The two bullets in the man's brain had not, they said, killed him. He was "murdered" by the physicians who removed his heart! This line of defense is encouraged by the fact that most states accept a definition of death, dating back to 1906, in which death is identified with the final cessation of heartbeat and respiration. In an effort to resolve such problems, the American Bar Association has recently approved a resolution from its Law and Medicine Committee urging acceptance of a legal definition of death as the "irreversible, total cessation of brain function."

It has been suggested that the medical profession has narrowed the competing definitions of death down to three major options:[5]

1. The moment at which irreversible destruction of brain matter, with no possibility of regaining consciousness, is conclusively determined.

2. The moment at which spontaneous heartbeat cannot be restored.

3. "Brain death" as determined by the EEG.

The inadequacy of each of these definitions is not difficult to spot. Consider the first one. When are we to conclude that we have witnessed "the moment" at which there is no possibility of restoring consciousness? It really ought not to be equated with the moment when we give up. When are we to know that there is no such possibility? What objective data would allow a conclusive determination that *now* (and not before) it is impossible for consciousness to be restored? Those elusive objective data are really what we are after. This definition is something like defining death as the moment at which it is conclusively determined that life will not be recovered. That may be true. But it is of little help.

The second definition carries with it a similar problem. Asking for "the moment at which spontaneous heartbeat cannot be restored'' is like asking for the moment at which the Dow Jones average failed to reach 1200. What moment was that? When are we entitled to conclude that a heartbeat cannot be restored? If a heart has stopped beating and two hours of solid effort to revive it have failed, it would appear that it was impossible to do so from the moment it stopped beating. If it can ever be restarted, then clearly it was possible to do so regardless of how long it has been. When is the moment of death? Again, the suggestion seems to be that the moment of death occurs when we stop trying to restore life. But the physician is interested in determining when he is entitled to quit, and this definition provides him with nothing.

We have already noted the difficulties presented by the third definition.

It really is not fair to be overly harsh with these definitions. We are admittedly in a period in which technology has outdistanced our understanding. It is always easier to tear down proposals than it is to offer better ones. But it is important to illustrate just where we stand, and we have run into a buzzsaw. The problem is that death may not be identifiable with any given moment. We are used to hearing of cases in which people have ''died,'' on the operating table or in the ocean or on a street corner, and then been brought back. In chapter 1 a distinction was made between death and dying. It was noted that dying is a process. Perhaps death, too, is a process.[6] In some sense we begin to die at the moment of conception. Socrates believed that the true philosopher is always pursuing death and dying. This would seem to be true of everyone. Death and dying may both be processes, or stages of a single process, distinguished at least in part by the fact that dying is a process, or that portion of the process, which occurs within the parameters of our earthly life, while death most certainly does not. It is true that certain life functions continue long after ''death'' by any reasonable definition has occurred. One of the more intriguing jobs of the undertaker is shaving the cadaver just prior to the viewing and making sure that the continuing growth of beard is concealed by a judicious use of makeup. There is, in fact, a good deal of life remaining in the "dead" body. The hair and fingernails continue to grow. Many of the cells of the body retain their ability to function and even reproduce for quite some time after the person has died. We may be faced with an insurmountable problem in trying to define death. About the only thing all medical authorities agree on as a sure sign of death is the presence of rigor mortis. But most would also agree that death has in fact taken place some time prior to that. At the moment we really have no better a medical definition of death than that provided by the United Nations Vital Statistics which defines death as the permanent loss of all signs of life, which sounds something like Augustine's definition of evil as the absence of good.

Perhaps we philosophers should tend to our own metaphysical knitting. Without discounting in the slightest the importance of developing a medical definition of death, we should recognize that our real interests lie elsewhere. Our concern is with the implications of death for the individual who must die. Our questions have to do with an understanding of the existential status of a person after death. It may be that, by paying closer attention to our philosophical interests, we might be able to formulate a working definition of death based upon these interests.

The mysteries of death, from the point of view of the philosopher, have to do with what happens to the mind. Philosophers have tended to divide into three main groups when considering the mind. There are those who insist that the mind is a myth—that the word "mind" really has no referent and therefore does not name anything. Other philosophers have held that the mind is either identical with, or completely a function of, the body—an epiphenomenon accompanying brain processes and totally dependent upon the workings of the brain. Still others believe that it makes sense to speak of the mind as a separate reality—a nonphysical substance which might exist apart from the body. If we simply identify the mind as consciousness, then we can quickly dismiss the first option. There is such a thing as consciousness, and therefore the word "mind" does have a referent. I cannot observe consciousness in other things, nor can I even observe it in myself in the usual sense of that word. But I cannot reasonably deny that I am aware. I do not eyeball my consciousness. But I can perceive it. I *am* my consciousness. It is pointless for me to attempt to convince another that I have a mind. If he does not believe that I am aware, there is little that I can do. Should the reader, with respect to himself, entertain any doubts along this line, he is directed to his own head.

That leaves us with two basic options. If we assume that mind, or consciousness, is real, it would seem that it is either totally dependent upon, or perhaps identical with, the body, or it is not. At this point it really does not matter which of these positions is the correct one. It should be possible to develop a working definition of death which can be compatible with either school of thought. We cannot, at this early stage, commit ourselves to an affirmation or a denial of the possibility of the mind's continuing to exist after death. But it is clear that death entails the absence of mental or conscious expression through the body. Whether or not there is a continuation of awareness apart from the body, the event of death implies that the physical body has lost the capacity to be aware. Perhaps this is because consciousness has disappeared, like a flame which is snuffed out. Or maybe it has gone on to better, or at least other, things. Either way, it is absent from the physical body. And this is really all we need in order to pursue the philosophical questions concerning death. Let us simply define death as the permanent absence of consciousness in a physical body.

The reader is forgiven if he feels disappointed. Our definition of death is something short of spectacular. It does not add a new page to the book of philosophical truth. It is of absolutely no use to the physician who is still wondering how to tell when his patient is dead. It is, in fact, subject to exactly the same criticisms we directed at the various medical definitions of death. But those criticisms were directed at the definitions as attempts to determine the moment of death, and that really is not our concern. It is the job of the philosopher not to determine the moment at which death occurs, but rather to identify what death, whenever it occurs, *is*. We wish the physician well, but we have metaphysical bones to pick. And this definition should serve us adequately. It is, after all, the status of the mind that most concerns the philosopher. Death is a threat precisely because it forces me to consider the possibility that the permanent absence of consciousness in my physical body, whenever it occurs, is equivalent to the permanent absence of my consciousness in any mode. The nothingness of death is the extinction of the mind.

It may occur to the reader that our definition of death as the permanent absence of consciousness in a physical body negates the possibility of recovering from death. It rejects the accuracy of speaking of a patient "dying" on the operating table and subsequently being brought back to life, since the absence of consciousness was not permanent. Attention-arresting titles such as "I Died at 10:52 A.M." [7] may belong to interesting and even insightful articles, but cannot count as legitimate examples of death. It is not denied that the experiences of those who have apparently died and then recovered are important. Such experiences may well prove to be significant in understanding the metaphysics of death. Perhaps, for example, the only distinction between the absence of consciousness in a physical body which is in a dreamless sleep or an extended coma or a momentary heart stoppage, and death itself, is the adjective "permanent." If this is true, then, although genuine death has not occurred, these experiences could very well provide insights into the nature of death.

It might be objected that our definition could apply to a brick. We do not normally think of inanimate objects as being dead, but surely there is a permanent absence of consciousness in the physical body of a brick. Are we committed to thinking of bricks and stones and dirt and the like as being dead? I believe the answer is yes. We could avoid this position by defining death as the permanent withdrawal of consciousness in a physical body, and there may be nothing wrong with that. But withdrawal seems to suggest a separable entity which can be removed from a substance. The mind may well be just such an entity, but that is an issue we should not settle prematurely. It is not so odd, either, to attribute death to inanimate objects. The phrase "dead as a doornail" indicates that we are not so wide of the mark.

What does our definition say about one who is in a prolonged coma? The answer is not clear. Two things must be settled before we can decide whether a person in a coma is dead. First, is there consciousness in the physical body of one in a coma? The comatose patient is said to be unconscious, but there is not an absence of consciousness if the patient is experiencing any sort of awareness at all—even dream awareness. It is difficult, perhaps impossible, to determine whether such an altered state of consciousness is present in a comatose patient, but if there is any form of awareness, then the patient is not dead. If there is no consciousness in such a patient, then we must ask whether this situation is permanent. That determination depends upon an adequate medical definition of the situation. If there is an irreversible absence of consciousness in a comatose patient, even if the body is kept functioning, then the patient is dead. The determination of whether this is the case depends upon the development of an acceptable medical definition of death.

It is, in fact, a commonsense definition of death that we have developed. It is neither daring nor startling nor particularly new. It simply expresses what most people mean by death without closing the door to various theories about what happens after death.

In attempting to define death we begin also to understand what is meant by life. Life as we know it involves the physical embodiment, or perhaps expression, of a mind or consciousness. Nonconscious things are nonliving things. Consciousness may be primitive or advanced, but without it there is no life. The amoeba is alive, and it would seem reasonable to attribute to the amoeba a certain primitive form of awareness. Plants are alive. Here the issue appears to be cloudy, but an ever-increasing body of data suggests a definite form of awareness in plants. We have experienced life only in a physical medium. Can there be life after death? We must insist that this may be possible. If it is possible for the mind to exist without the body, then life after death is also a possibility. It may not be possible for the mind to exist apart from a body, but we really do not know that yet. It is clear now that our definition of life is, quite simply, consciousness. And what could be more reasonable than that?

CHAPTER 3
The Soul

Having developed a more or less adequate definition of death which should serve our philosophical interests, we should not hesitate to turn boldly to the task of defining the soul. It is, as we have suggested, the soul which contains the mysteries of death. Death is a philosophical puzzle only in conjunction with the assumption that there might be an aspect, or an element, about us which could conceivably survive the death of the body. This implies that there might be something more than body in our makeup. This would be the soul. Should we assume that we do not have a soul, it would seem that the most intriguing questions raised by death are answered. If the human animal is understood as precisely the physical creature that we can observe via our senses, and nothing more, then we can say with some confidence that the metaphysics of death is an illegitimate area of study. There is nothing "meta" about it. To the extent that the self is equated with the physical body, we *know* what death is. It is really nothing more than the breakdown of a machine. We could easily make an analogy with an automobile which refuses to start (although our choice of an automobile for the analogy rather than, say, an electric dynamo, tends to stack the deck). If we can repair the automobile and get it going again, we can prolong the life of the vehicle. If the breakdown is so extensive as to be beyond our ability to effect repairs, the automobile has "died." Death would then be understood as the breakdown of the physical body, and the inability to get it going again. Just as a dead automobile will quickly disintegrate into its ultimate components, the dead body immediately begins to decay, separating into the various elements which once formed it. A dead automobile will be recycled into new metal or rusty puddles. So, too, a dead body is recycled into plant fertilizer or dusty ashes in a coffin. If that is what death is all about, then philosophy should turn its attention to other things. And it is certainly possible that death is just that—the irreparable breakdown of the body and the subsequent degeneration of decay.

But is that not the issue? There are genuine mysteries in death because we are not at all sure that we are organic automobiles. The automobile serves its purpose as a vehicle for the driver. (This is why the choice of an automobile for the analogy stacked the deck.) Perhaps our bodies serve a similar purpose. It is possible that we are analogous not to the automobile, but to the automobile and its driver. If so, the obvious breakdown of the machine we call our body would no more entail our complete extinction than the failure of an automobile means the passing of its owner. If there is something of us which survives death, it would be what has been called the soul.

In attempting to define the soul, we are immersing ourselves in very muddy waters. There are few things quite as confusing as the concept of the soul. One of my more perverted forms of amusement is asking students whether they believe in the soul and what they mean by that term. Generally, the student will profess some belief in the soul, but strongly resist any efforts to get him to explain the concept as he understands it. But I am nothing if I am not persistent, and I pursue the student like a philosophical hound, encouraging him to give it his best shot. The answers are nearly always embarrassing. The reluctance of most people to discuss their concept of the soul is quite understandable. I have heard otherwise sophisticated students struggling with the most inane definitions of their souls imaginable. At the end of a rather lengthy period of more or less gentle prodding on my part, one of my better students finally agreed to try and express what she meant by the term ''soul.'' The conversation went like this:

"Well, I think that the soul is an image of yourself."

"An image?"

"Yes, your soul looks like you."

"How does it differ from me?"

"Well, it's smaller."

"Is it like a little portrait of me? Or a statue? Or . . ."

"No, no!'' (Irritation—justified, of course.) "The soul is . . . Well, I think of it as a kind of smoky image. It looks like the person, and I suppose it would be inside the body."

"A little smoky copy of me, inside my body?"

"Well, I guess so . . . I don't know!"

I wanted desperately to ask her just where in my body this little smoke resided, but I had already pushed her a bit far. The student was embarrassed. She realized that her explanation of the soul sounded silly, but that was the best she could do. And if the truth were known, probably most people think of the soul as a little "Casper the friendly ghost" running, or floating, around their brains. It is a similar reasoning which has prompted certain suggestions as to how we might determine whether or not we have a soul. One man claimed that it could be done if we took a dying patient into a carefully sealed room. After death has occurred a close examination of the room should reveal a small crack somewhere if the soul has escaped, as it presumably does at death. Still others are working with the idea of weighing the dying patient in a set of highly sensitive scales. If death involves the loss of the soul from the body, so this reasoning goes, then it should be revealed in a minuscule, but measurable, loss of weight which cannot be accounted for otherwise. I have heard of two such experiments which produced contradictory results. I should expect that these and similar experiments would yield a negative result. They are clearly predicated upon the notion that the soul is some sort of gauzy, filmy substance of a corporeal nature. The soul must literally break through the walls of a sealed room, thereby producing a little crack somewhere. The soul, if we have one, must weigh something, and is therefore quantifiable by weight and perhaps by volume. The assumption seems to be that reality is corporeal; therefore the soul, if it is real, must be corporeal.

This assumption has its roots in deepest antiquity. We have already noted the concept of the soul held by the Greek and Roman atomists. They viewed the soul as being formed from the atoms of reality, no different in this respect from any other existing thing. Many traditions have held that the soul must escape the body at death through one of the orifices of the body, slithering out as best it can through whatever opening is handy. This belief is said to have produced a tendency in some cultures to cover tightly the mouth and nose of the dying person in hopes of keeping the soul from making good its escape. At least so I am told. Several American Indian tribes have understood the soul as an animated doll, resembling the physical body of the person whose soul it is. The Nootka, for example, believed that the soul was a little guy standing up inside your head, helping you to keep your balance and determine your direction. At least one Australian tribe was in the habit of placing glowing coals in the ears and nose of the dead in order to avoid being haunted by the ghost inside the dead person's body. Many people have believed that sleep is a period of time during which the soul might well decide to venture out of the body. The Tibetans have long accepted this as a form of the very natural process of "astral-projection," a method of projecting one's conscious awareness out of the body. The Transylvanians, on the other hand, thought it unacceptable for the soul to enjoy such nocturnal freedom and so trained their children to sleep with their mouths closed.

The concept of the soul as some variation on the theme of a smoky Casper the friendly ghost is a common one. My student need not have felt embarrassed. In fact, while we might smile at such primitive notions, it is a bit difficult to do any better. Most of us entertain more or less sophisticated versions of the idea that the soul is a piece of smoke. But what are the options? We are not, presumably, to take seriously the ancient identifications of the soul with blood or breath or heat or one's shadow. Such concepts were acceptable at an early period of our cultural development. But they do not have the ring of truth today. Little ghosts and goblins are even more unsatisfying. Perhaps the most reasonable position would be to agree with those who deny the reality of the soul. We might suppose that an enlightened philosophy would dismiss the idea of the soul as the product of primitive thought.

In the *Phaedo,* Plato's dialogue presenting the death of Socrates, considerable thought is given to the concept of the soul. As one might expect from a philosopher about to drink the hemlock, Socrates considers various arguments dealing with the possibility that the soul might survive death. It is often the case that students find themselves somewhat puzzled over the fact that Socrates does not seem to take seriously his obligation, first of all, to argue that there *is* a soul. He apparently assumes the existence of the soul and proceeds from there to discuss its nature and its destiny. But if one can understand what Socrates means by the soul it will be clear that any argument for its existence would be superfluous. Socrates apparently understands the soul to be a sort of life principle or, perhaps more loosely, life itself. Is it not the case, asks Socrates, that "whatever be the object upon which the soul lays hold, she invariably comes to it bringing life?" [1] The soul would seem to

44

be that which, when added to any physical substance, produces a living thing. Conversely, the soul is that which, when subtracted from any physical substance, produces the condition of death. It is the missing element in the cadaver. Socrates seems to be suggesting that the soul is consciousness. It is what we mean by the mind.

Philosophy of mind has had a curious history. Unlike earlier identifications of the mind, or soul, with various physical substances such as blood or fire or atoms, Socrates' view of the soul was that it was completely nonphysical in nature. It is opposed to the physical and is therefore not to be identified with the body or any part of it. This was a startling new concept for philosophy, but it was quickly picked up and expanded upon by later thinkers.

Some of the clearest thinking in this area was done by Descartes. Descartes was convinced that philosophy should cultivate a radical doubt if it is ever to hope to discover truth. Only when a proposition cannot reasonably be doubted are we entitled to accept it. Descartes found that, by supposing that there might be a demonic power similar to God but without his goodness, he could develop the strongest possible argument for skepticism. He never really believed that there was such an evil demon, but until he could show there was not, he felt obligated to acknowledge it as a possibility. It would seem that Descartes had thereby destroyed any hope of knowing anything at all. He could be subject to the deceptions of powers far beyond his comprehension. He could therefore be mistaken in all his beliefs. He might or might not have a body; he might or might not be sitting in front of a fireplace writing his meditations; the perceptions which came to him might not be valid. He was even able to doubt the truths of mathematics. The powers of an evil demon might be such as to deceive him in whatever matters Descartes could consider. There might not be such a demon. But

45

then again, there might be. The troubles of this world even provide some reason to believe that such might be the case. The hypothesis of an evil demon allowed Descartes to doubt even the most obvious "truths." To the extent that such a being is possible it would appear that all our intellectual discoveries and beliefs are condemned to possess a quality of uncertainty. I cannot be sure. I may be deceived. I cannot trust what I believe. I may be correct, but I may be mistaken. I . . . I . . . I . . . At this point Descartes began to consider the status of the doubter himself. Who, or what, is this "I"? Is it not the case that, whether I am deceived or not, I must necessarily exist so long as I am able to wonder?

Descartes now develops what may be the strongest argument ever presented in any discipline. It is famous enough to be found on the walls of some of the finer public restrooms. I have seen it printed in wet cement. It is Descartes' well-known dictum, *Cogito, ergo sum.* I think, therefore I am (or as one student, I hope as the result of a typographical error, put it: I thing, therefore I am). Descartes is saying that there is simply no way an individual can reasonably doubt his own existence. Even under the deception of an evil demon I must exist as one who is deceived. Regardless of how mistaken I may be in my thinking, *that* I think cannot be doubted. Descartes has presented a strong argument for skepticism—the strongest ever devised. He believes that there is no possible hypothesis which would allow for a greater doubt than the existence of an all-powerful deceiver. And yet, even if this massive deception should be the case, Descartes cannot doubt his own existence. He is still able to doubt everything else. He cannot be sure that the world is as it appears. He does not know that he has a physical body, or, if he has, that it is the body he believes it to be. He cannot even accept mathematics at this point. It is hard to see how two plus two could equal anything but four, but the powers of the evil demon may conceivably extend even to Descartes' understanding of mathematics.

What has Descartes shown? Some would say "nothing." If he cannot be sure even of mathematics or the fact of his own body, he has really established nothing at all. And yet this is surely mistaken. Descartes knows that he exists—at least as "thinking substance." He may also exist as a physical body, but he is not yet sure. Two plus two may after all equal four, but he is not yet sure. What Descartes has done is to show that our knowledge of our own awareness is absolutely indubitable. He has shown that it is far more certain than our knowledge of anything physical or even mathematical. He has, in fact, demonstrated the existence of the soul. I cannot escape knowing that I have a mind, because the knowing process itself is mental. I may have a body. My mind may even be totally dependent on my body. But my mind is not identical with my body. At least it is not identical with my body if we understand body to be physical, extended substance. This is obvious for the simple reason that, if my mind is identical with physical substance, then Descartes' success in establishing the certainty of his mind should have been tantamount to a demonstration of his body. Yet it clearly was not. He is consistently able to affirm that he has (or is) a mind while he continues to wonder whether he has a body. If I am the object of the deceptions of an evil demon, then I must exist at least as one who is deceived. If I am not deceived, then I must exist as one who is not deceived. If I am sometimes deceived and sometimes not deceived, then again, I must exist at least so long as I am aware.

What, then, *is* the mind? It is not enough simply to affirm the existence of something. We must be able to say something about it. What is this Cartesian "thinking substance?" Descartes insists that it is not identical with physical, or extended, substance. The strong tendency in most students of philosophy is to equate the mind with the brain. But the brain is certainly an example of extended substance. It has weight and volume. It has shape and color. It can be painted green or thrown at a wall or hung up to dry. But the mind seems not to have such properties. What color is the mind? What is the shape of awareness? How much does consciousness weigh? Does a living body weigh a bit more than a dead body because of its additional attribute of consciousness? I am told that Einstein's brain is in a jar at Princeton. But where is his mind? If the mind is identical with the brain, then it too must be in that jar. But that is silly. We really do not know where Einstein's mind is, or even *if* it is, but I would bet that it is not in any jar. The mind, then, seems best described *via negativa*—through a process of negation. It is not extended. It has no mass. It cannot be spatially located. It is not quantifiable, etc. But this is not enough, since the same things could be said about nothing—i.e., that which does not exist is not extended, nor does it have any other of the properties associated with physical reality. But the mind is not nothing. What then is it? It appears that we can at the moment do no better than to say that it is consciousness. It is awareness. The mind has what might be called a metaphysical self-reflexive quality about it. It is able to know itself in a unity of subject and object. Our knowledge that we are aware has a certainty about it that we cannot hope to achieve in anything else. We know our minds because we *are* our minds. I am, at least in part, a mind. But what I am does not appear to be similar to what this page of print is. I happen to be some kind of thinking substance and therefore I not only am, I *know* that I am. In this I have slightly the advantage of this page of print.

How, then, am I related to my body? I seem somehow to be "laced" throughout this tube of flesh, even if I am not identical with it. At this point Descartes raises, for the torment not only of himself but all of subsequent philosophy, one of the most puzzling of all philosophical issues. It is known as the Mind/Body Problem. It is a real problem, and we cannot avoid it. But we can postpone it. Our purpose in this chapter is simply to argue for the position that the soul is the mind and that the mind is real, whatever it is.

Have we resurrected Casper? Are we seriously committed to a doctrine Gilbert Ryle ridicules as "the ghost in the machine"? The answer is a qualified no. We are not, for example, committed to the dualism of Cartesian philosophy. That is, we may, as Ryle does, hold an identity theory of mind and body. But this identity cannot be located in physical substance. However cleverly we manipulate the terminology, whenever we begin taking seriously the possibility of any entity existing in a nonphysical sense, we invite charges of intellectual nonsense. But we have illustrious company. Philosophy is not alone in its dealings with things nonphysical. Does there exist a prime number between one and three? Of course. The nonphysical status of the number two seems hardly to produce the slightest disturbance among mathematicians. Nor does it seem to elicit charges of unscientific ghostliness. Mathematicians have long been satisfied to work among entities which have none of the properties of physical substances. Do numbers exist? Are they real? Well, *is* there a prime number between one and three or is there not? But then, the association between philosophy and mathematics has always been suspiciously close. Euclid, Pythagoras, Descartes, and Russell have waffled in their allegiance between philosophy and mathematics. Even Plato was moved to place over the door of his academy the warning, "Let no one enter who is ignorant of mathematics."

Let us, then, consider physics. What are the latest theories of the physicist as to the ultimate nature of reality? Certainly they bear little resemblance to Newtonian marbles. It is not particles, but waves—or perhaps wavicles. Or it is vectors. Or perhaps it is concentrations of gravitational forces, or maybe twists and crinkles in the substance of space/time. Or maybe, as one physicist has stated, "It's just mathematics, that's all." The ancient Pythagoreans may have been right all along! Even the supposedly discredited doctrine of the aether is being resurrected under the guise of such terms as "sub-aether" or "dispersive medium." [2] Physics, that concrete science of hard stuff, has been forced to abandon even the concept of an ultimate particle. Milič Čapek, a philosopher with strong interest and training in physics, warns us that "the extent of the contemporary crisis in physics cannot be fully grasped if we do not realize that the very concept of *substance* or *thinghood* has become questionable." [3]

My doctoral dissertation required me to deal in depth with the concept of a "necessary being," an entity which could not possibly fail to exist, something like a triangle cannot possibly fail to have three sides. It occurred to me that the quality of necessity seemed more appropriate to mathematics, tautologies, and axioms than to things. I went to some lengths to define the concept of a being so as to preclude the possibility that a necessary being might be something as abstract as the Pythagorean theorum or pi or the like. It appears now that my efforts in this direction might have been misguided. Some rather respectable scholars are seriously toying with the notion that the ultimate nature of reality might very well be found, not in any elemental particle, but rather in the laws which govern such particles. Physicist Allen D. Allen states this position most bravely: "The chair on which you are sitting is constructed out of fundamental laws, rather than out of such material objects as atomic particles—an almost theological concept." [4] This approach promises to resolve one of the more intractable problems in philosophy of religion, namely the issue between those who believe that God, as the ultimate explanation of the whole of reality (including himself), must be understood as a necessary being, and those who have insisted, quite reasonably, that necessity can never be predicated of beings in the normal sense of the term "being" (i.e., thing or object), but can only be applied to mathematical propositions, tautologies, and similar abstractions. Perhaps the truth embraces both schools of thought. Ultimate reality may finally be an abstraction, but no less real (or ultimate!) for that.

The point being made here is simply that philosophers and theologians are not the only ones who deal with abstractions. There is an increasing body of evidence which suggests that the final pursuit of all truth will end with a convergence upon ultimate, mind-blowing abstractions rather than elemental bits of Newtonian world-stuff.

Now who is kidding whom? Is philosophy to feel shamed because it accepts the reality of the one thing we cannot doubt? Are we to hang our heads because we take seriously the mind, while mathematicians cavort among numbers and physicists brazenly speak of psi-fields?

Our suggestion that the mind be taken seriously as something "real" is not as radical or careless as one might initially suspect. The concept of mind presented here is incompatible only with the kind of naïve materialism associated with nineteenth-century physics. It has not been denied here that the mind is identical with the body, unless the body is understood as Newtonian substance. No commitment has been made as to the possibility that the mind might exist without the body. The mind may be totally dependent upon the body. The death of the body may entail the death of the mind. Perhaps the mind, as Thomas Henry Huxley believed, is an epiphenomenon of the brain, accompanying brain process as a shadow follows the body. There are shadows. They therefore have some kind of reality. But they do not have independent existence. Something similar may be true of the mind. But consciousness is at least as real as shadows, and certainly no less real than numbers. Its precise existential status as a substantial reality has not yet been determined. But it is something which can be considered by philosophy. It is the soul. We have actually developed a rather conservative and cautious definition of the soul.

Having defined the soul as the mind, we must defend that identity. There should be some compelling reasons for us to accept the equation of the soul and mind. But it seems that the best reason we can give for defining the soul as the mind is simply that all other options are less satisfying. We must choose, first of all, whether or not the soul is worth defining. There are those who are inclined to relegate the concept of the soul to the outer darkness of myths and superstitions. They would deny that it makes any sense to talk about a soul. We have obviously rejected that position. Having decided to retain the term, we must define it, choosing among the various options available. It would be too clever to choose among options which are not available. How shall we proceed? Identifications of the soul with blood or heat or breath are not reasonable options for our time. What about spirit? Christian theology has, in fact, defined the soul as spiritual substance. We might be more in line with traditional and contemporary theology by defining the soul as spirit. But what is spirit? What *is* spirit if not mind? We hear people speaking of physical, mental, and spiritual health. A guest lecturer in one of my classes, a prominent rabbi, once addressed himself to the concept of spiritual health. He talked also about the powers of prayer as spiritual telepathy. When I questioned him as to whether he made a distinction between spiritual and mental, he appeared to be genuinely puzzled. His response finally was, "I don't know. Sometimes I do, and sometimes I don't." And then he went on. I have never been able to get a handle on that distinction. Can a person be physically and mentally healthy and spiritually sick? Perhaps this is possible. But the distinction between the mental and the spiritual continues to escape me.

Further, the identification of the soul with consciousness has some positive advantages. It lends itself directly to the prime issues in the philosophy of death. We might have simply defined the soul with the whole person and let it go at that. But we are interested in the question of personal survival. If the soul is identified with the whole person, including his physical body, then we should be quite puzzled as to just what might be meant by the concept of survival of death. Few people take seriously the idea that we will survive in precisely the same physical forms we now have. If there is personal survival it most likely will be on the mental plane. Any idea of survival without awareness does not provide what we are looking for. The mystery of death is exactly the question of the ongoing consciousness of an individual. Our identification of the soul with the mind provides us with just the definition that is needed in order to pursue the philosophical questions about death. The body obviously survives in terms of its basic elements. It decays in form, but not in substance. And who really cares, anyway? We can surely bring ourselves to accept the passing of the body. Our concern is with the destiny of our awareness. Do our minds disappear or cease functioning upon the death of the body, or not? The immortality of the soul is a question dealing with the mind.

The definition of soul as mind, then, is quite simply the best of the available alternatives. It avoids the unsatisfactory associations of the soul with various physical substances such as moisture or one's footprints or even the entire body. It focuses our attention upon the real issues of death. And it begins to clarify our understanding of the self. We are, after all, aware. We do not know why or how. But we are absolutely certain that no system of physics or metaphysics or cosomological speculation into the nature of reality can be acceptable which fails to provide an adequate account of consciousness. In developing a satisfactory model of physics we cannot neglect the mind. It simply will not do to develop a conceptual framework of reality which does not include the conceptual process itself. The German physicist Erwin Schrödinger has said that, in the attempt to understand the world, "consciousness is absolutely fundamental." If this is true of physics, how much more is it the case in philosophy, and especially in our speculations on death? If we are accused of a sort of contemporary witchcraft in our intentions to study a ghost in the machine, we can only note that twentieth-century intellectual disciplines harbor a number of ghosts in their closets. Perhaps they are legitimate. Perhaps not. In any case, it is surely time to let them out and determine whether they can survive in the light of truth. If they cannot, let truth be their exorcist.

CHAPTER 4
Death as a Uniquely Human Event

"All men are mortal." It is difficult to argue with that observation, but one might wonder just how profound it is. All men are mortal. But so are all caterpillars. Daisies are mortal, too. Death is not the special prerogative of the human species. It belongs to the plant and animal kingdoms as well. We have no particular monopoly on mortality. Death comes to giant tortoises and California redwoods, to the lilies of the field and the birds of the air, to the good, the bad, the beautiful, and the ugly. In a moment of carelessness we might even be inclined to say that death is an inescapable feature of all life. But we would be wrong. At least we would not quite be correct. There are some living things which appear to enjoy a quality of immortality.

Two California scientists have recently announced the discovery of a strain of bacteria, as yet unidentified, which was still viable after having been frozen for at least ten thousand years. (Some estimates range up to one million years!) The little things were thawed out, and some of them promptly began doing what comes naturally—reproducing. Such behavior from a one-million-year-old creature is quite startling, to say the least. But then, they did cheat. They existed in a state of suspended animation below the permafrost of Antarctica, and that is not really the kind of immortality we covet. Nearer the mark is WPN-114, the oldest known living thing. WPN-114, known to its friends as "Methuselah," is estimated to be from forty-five hundred to forty-nine hundred years old and has recently become the proud parent of forty-eight offspring. Methuselah is a bristle-cone pine tree, and Methuselah has been alive throughout recorded history. But such facts generate only mild interest among those who have set their sights on the question of immortality. Even creatures whose life-spans range upward of one million years cannot properly be called immortal.

The quality of immortality might more appropriately be attributed to another of nature's wonders whose life-span seems to have no limit. These creatures exist at a rather low level of sophistication as we define it, but they command our admiration—even a measure of envy—in at least this respect. They do not die. I am speaking, of course, about the amoeba. It is possible that the first amoeba is in some sense still alive. Because the amoeba reproduces by cellular division (fission), it manages to avoid death. When a single amoeba divides into two amoebas they both go their separate ways, and try as you might, you will not find a dead amoeba left over. They may not have as much fun, but this method of reproduction does have its compensations.

It is not clear whether this is genuine immortality. Assuming that the original amoeba was a distinct aware entity, the analysis of just what has happened when "it" becomes "them" is a bit of a puzzle. Has one consciousness produced another? Then we should be able to point to one of the amoebas and identify it as the original one. But this immediately strikes us as an exercise in futility. The original guy was simply cut in half and that is all there is to it. It would be arbitrary to single out one of the resulting pair as the one that did the dividing. Perhaps, in the process of division, the consciousness of the orignal amoeba is divided along with the substance of his amoeba-body. But it is difficult to understand the concept of a division in consciousness. How can awareness be divided? If it can, we begin to violate one of the more interesting arguments for immortality, based upon the notion that the soul, or consciousness, is simple and therefore indestructible. We might say "So much for that argument," but we should be able to explain the psychic dynamics involved. Perhaps it is better, for the moment at least, to allow the amoeba its immortality and let it go at that.

The enigma of the amoeba might lead us to suggest that the ability to die is an achievement of evolution. Mortality can be understood as one of the marks of advanced life-forms. It is a dubious honor. It is not easy to avoid casting a longing glance at the lowliest of creatures. But it does appear that one of the first qualities that life strives toward is death. Curiouser and curiouser . . .

The supposed immortality of the amoeba is scant consolation to us. Even less satisfying is the suggestion that our ability to die is a sign of our relative superiority to the amoeba. It still gets the last laugh, and we are not appeased knowing that it cannot even smile. The amoeba is only an exception to the general rule of death. And when the sun finally grows cold, even the proud amoeba is doomed. Our rendezvous with death is a trial that is ultimately shared by all living things, and the fact that we share a common destiny is only mildly interesting.

But we would be superficial if we did not acknowledge a feeling that there is something special about our situation. Death comes to all creatures, but it has a unique quality for human beings. Camus boldly stated that for man "there is but one truly serious philosophical problem, and that is suicide." [1] We do not have a choice about whether we will die. We share the fate of all living things. But we are alone in being able to choose whether we shall die by our own hand. We alone can decide at any time to hasten the inevitable, thereby cheating fate to some small degree by determining the moment of our own death. This ability gives some indication of the uniqueness of our position. We can, by our own will, choose death. It may be argued that this is not unique to man, since a number of animals have been observed to commit suicide en masse. But suicide is not a lemming-like action. It is not comparable to a school of whales beaching themselves in shallow water, or horses rushing madly into a burning barn. Suicide is the deliberate choosing of death. It would be ludicrous to defend the idea that the lemming is consciously choosing to die as he plunges into the sea. The supposition that animals even understand that they will die can be defended only by those who are playing philosophical games. We do not know what goes on in the lemming mind when he checks out, but surely it is not something along the line of "good-bye, cruel world." Animals may encounter other dead animals in their experience, but we have no reason to suppose that they have any understanding of their own eventual fate.

Suicide, understood as the conscious choosing of death, is possible in man only because man alone knows that he is going to die. Suicide is unique to man. But it is man's knowledge of death as a personal inevitability that makes suicide possible. We are able to abstract, from our experience of death in others, the implications of death for ourselves. The ability to do that may not make us any happier, but it does set us apart. It is our knowledge, our certainty that we are going to die, that gives death a unique quality for human creatures. All men *are* mortal. And only human beings know that. Our concern with death is far more than a variation of the instinct for survival. We alone are aware of the implications should we fail to survive. Dim and inadequate as our understanding of death is, the mere fact that I know that one day there will be a permanent absence of consciousness in my physical body places me a quantum distance from other living species as I know them.

But I intend to argue that there is something even more basically unique to man than our ability to commit suicide or our knowledge that death is our eventual lot. If we can imagine a scale of life, a continuum from the most primitive form of consciousness to the most advanced, the point can be made that man's position on that scale involves a very unique status with regard to death. I will open myself up to the charge of anthropomorphic arrogance by suggesting that man does not occupy the very lowest point on that continuum. I am not sure just what does qualify as the most basic, or primitive, form of consciousness. I am inclined to suspect that it may not be the amoeba. The astronomer Firsoff has postulated the existence of elementary particles of mind stuff—"mindons." Perhaps something like these occupy the initial points on our scale. We do not know just what counts as the first level of consciousness, but I should be allowed to deny that it is man. Humility is a fine attribute, but the sophistication of the human mind is too obvious for us to place ourselves at the foot of this table. I would, in fact, place human consciousness rather further along toward the other end of the spectrum.

But not at the very end. If it is a mistake to place the human mind at the very lowest level of sophistication, it should be equally obvious that we do not belong at the highest level. It may be that we represent the most advanced form of consciousness we have yet encountered—and I would rather not talk about the dolphin. But it would certainly be folly to suppose that what we are is anything like the most advanced form of consciousness possible. If the reader believes in God, then the issue is settled. God takes his proper seat at the head of this table. But even the nonbeliever will have a difficult time defending the notion that man should take that seat. Are there higher forms of mind in the universe? It is almost certainly the case that there are. Reality is just too large, too incredibly vast, and has been around too long for us to take seriously the idea that an insignificant ball of warm mud orbiting an average size star in a very unexceptional solar system located in a far corner of one of hundreds of thousands of galaxies in the visible universe sports the highest and most advanced form of mental reality. "Man is the most advanced creature in the universe!" We cannot even say it without smiling. Indeed, it is something of an effort just to spit it out without breaking into laughter. Such a phrase presents a *reductio ad absurdum* argument against itself. It is likely that there are beings far more advanced mentally than we. I am not thinking of technological advancement. There might well be races of beings whose level of technology vastly exceeds our own, yet who would occupy a position equivalent to ours on the scale of mental sophistication. I am thinking of the possibility of beings who may have evolved on a conscious level to the extent that we would stand in relationship to them as the amoeba stands to us. There is simply no reason, beyond the desires of our own egos, to deny such a possibility. We represent a certain stage of development rather more advanced than the amoeba. But we do ourselves no honor when we arbitrarily seat ourselves at the head of the table. We simply have no good reason to define ourselves as the most sophisticated form of mental existence possible.

But the fact is that we really do not know that such higher forms exist. I would perhaps be willing to put the rent money on there being such entities, but I most certainly would not stake my life on it. For our purposes, however, it does not matter whether in fact such life forms exist. It is only necessary to insist that they are possible. It is difficult to imagine just what a more advanced level of mind would be like, having experienced only our own form of consciousness and making more or less reasonable guesses at what is going on in our pet dog and the amoeba. But let us press on.

The position of man on the spectrum of mental sophistication would seem to provide him with a very unique status with respect to death. Death comes to us as an interesting combination of knowledge and mystery, a combination probably experienced by no other life-form. We are distinguished from the lower points on the continuum because, as we have already seen, we know that we are to die and they do not. We have, therefore, already begun to take the first steps toward understanding death. We have discovered that death is a part of our nature, and that has yet to be learned at the lower levels. There is, then, an element of knowledge that we have gained about death. We are not really totally ignorant about death if we have discovered our own mortality. With respect to what we know about death we are clearly unique when compared to the less sophisticated forms of mental reality.

But in this regard we would not be unique when compared to whatever higher forms of consciousness there might be. Certainly what little we know about death would not be lost at a more advanced stage. Nevertheless we should be distinguished from such higher beings, not in our knowledge, but in our ignorance. The assumption here is that an advanced form of consciousness would have made discoveries on the metaphysical plane. We may milk our technological achievements for all they are worth and yet be quite primitive in our understanding of ultimate reality. Further, it would seem that until certain metaphysical questions about the mind are answered with something more than mere speculation, we are blocked from any genuine possibility of what might be called an advanced stage of consciousness. The piling up of successes in the mechanical sphere does not at all imply a greater sophistication of the mental. If it is possible for there to exist advanced forms of mind beyond our own, it would be reasonable to understand this as a metaphysical advancement. Such levels of consciousness would presumably have made discoveries which go beyond any mechanical cleverness. I am suggesting that some, or all, of the mysteries of death would have been resolved. The mysteries of death are intrinsically related to the mysteries of the mind. To the extent that we cultivate a greater understanding of the mind, we must necessarily be resolving the puzzles of death. Whatever forms of advanced mental realities there are, or might be, would certainly enjoy a higher level of understanding of death than that attained by human creatures.

Man, then, would appear to have a fascinatingly unique relationship to death, one that may be a function of his evolutionary status in the spectrum of mental sophistication. The lower forms of life do not understand death, and in this respect our own lack of understanding is not unique. But neither do they confront death. They are not aware of their own finitude. We are. Whatever higher forms of life there may be, whether understood as advanced beings of another world, or angels, or God, would likely have discovered the very answers we seek. They would presumably understand death, certainly to a significantly greater extent than we do. At our level alone is death a significant mystery. Below us there is no mystery simply because there is no question. Above us there is no mystery because the questions have been answered. Again, it must be stressed that we are thinking of "above" in an evolutionary rather than a technological sense. Our confrontation with death is unique. Our ignorance is shared by the more primitive levels, our very limited knowledge is shared by the more advanced levels. But it would appear that our particular combination of ignorance and knowledge is not shared at any other level. Death is really a uniquely human problem.

There is some indication that our understanding of the spectrum of consciousness as linear may not be accurate. We have noted that organisms which reproduce by fission seem to possess a quality of immortality. We have also relegated them to the very lowest portions of the spectrum. There are many who believe that the very highest forms of consciousness—for example, God or Brahman or Cosmic Consciousness—are also immortal. In other words, there is a possible relationship between the very lowest and the very highest elements on our spectrum. The interesting thing is that this leads us to suspect that the two "ends" of the spectrum may not be as far apart as we might at first suppose. In fact it is often the case that what seem to be polar opposites are better understood as two sides of the same coin. In political ideology, for example, we find apparent opposition in the extreme positions taken by the left and right wings. But it takes no great cleverness to notice that there is a remarkable similarity even between two such strange bedfellows as these. The rhetoric is curiously similar. One group attacks the Military-Industrial Complex, while the other speaks darkly of the International Communist Conspiracy. There is a strong tendency on both sides to resort to broad brushes as they seek to label friend and foe. Many observers have noted the common impulse toward simplistic answers to complex questions. There is a fascinating similarity in terms of the quality of intolerance in both groups. Neither side seems willing to listen to the opinions of those with whom they disagree. The total devotion of the psyche to some vaguely defined cause which easily assumes cosmic significance is a mark of most extreme elements in the political scene. And so on. No one is suggesting that such positions are identical, but there are obvious similarities which go deep. Awareness of them can sometimes bring about a measure of understanding in a scene that might otherwise appear to be sheer chaos.

Another, perhaps more satisfying, example of the meeting of opposites is provided by astronomy. What is the greatest possible distance from one point to another? If certain theories of curved space are correct we are required to believe that it is right in back of the original point. The greatest possible distance I can travel, cosmically speaking, may be bounded by my point of origin. In traversing the breadth of an Einsteinian universe, I should end up just where I started, without ever having turned back or retraced my steps. Thus, in an admittedly odd sense, the greatest distance may be identical with no distance at all, or so it would seem.

Philosophy has hinted at something similar to this ever since Heraclitus boldly declared, more than twenty-five hundred years ago, that "opposition unites," and "life and death, and waking and sleeping, and youth and old age, are the same."[2] In metaphysics, Hegel and others have insisted that, when properly understood, Being and Nonbeing are the same thing. Here, of course, we hear echos of what most Oriental philosophers have been saying for centuries. The Hindu concept of the self (Atman) is said to be identical with God (Brahman). But this identity is found in the union of the ego, which is nonbeing or negation, with the absolute, which is Being-Itself. This theory is finding an increasingly sympathetic ear in the Western Christian tradition. There is a long history of Christian mysticism in which the distinction between God and the deepest levels of the self are blurred. Paul Tillich has insisted that the proper concept of God is precisely Being-Itself, or the ground of our own individual being. Teilhard de Chardin, a Jesuit paleontologist, identifies a unification principle in an expanded view of evolution based on an increasing complexity of all matter. God is understood in what must be recognized as a Hegelian concept of an absolute spirit or mind which is moving toward a cosmic realization (Point Omega) of its own essential nature through a pan-evolutionary process. It is not too much to say that some of the most exciting work in metaphysics and theology today is being done by those who take seriously the age-old vision of the unity of opposites.

There is even some suggestion of this in the paradoxical words of Jesus. "If any one would be first, he must be last of all" (Mark 9:35b). "Whoever receives me, receives not me but him who sent me" (Mark 9:37b). "Whoever would be great among you must be your servant, and whoever would be first among you must be slave of all'' (Mark 10:43b-44). ''For every one who exalts himself will be humbled, and he who humbles himself will be exalted'' (Luke 14:11). ''He who finds his life will lose it, and he who loses his life for my sake will find it'' (Matthew 10:39). It would be pure eisegesis to claim on the basis of such passages that Jesus was a Hegelian, or indeed any kind of metaphysical monist. But it should be clear that the sense of unity in apparent opposites is not entirely alien to Christian doctrine.

Our understanding of the self from physics, psychology, and philosophy seems to be moving in a similar direction. The suggestion of a metaphysical interrelatedness of all things, proclaimed by mystics across the centuries, and suggested by Einstein's relativity theories, seems to be confirmed by some recent studies in physics, especially in the areas of particle theory and field theory. We recognize various levels of existence from the most basic of elements through the pre-life inorganic compounds to the most primitive protoplasmic levels of life itself and beyond to whatever levels of sophistication mind is capable of achieving. But we may be making a conceptual mistake if we understand these forms of existence as unrelated or arranged in an aristocratic hierarchy such that the ''opposite'' ends are so remote from each other as to make them discontinuous. Suppose, even in this metaphysical analysis of being itself, that there is something so basic and so intrinsic to *all* of existence that the polar ends of the continuum of existence bend toward each other. What might this thread, this ground of existence, be? We cannot yet say with any certainty, but some interesting speculations are being made. We have long acknowledged that the quality of awareness, or consciousness, is shared throughout the animal kingdom. With very few exceptions (such as Descartes, who considered nonhuman animals to be unconscious automata) we have allowed animals to share with us our most important quality. We are conscious and so are they. But what about other forms of life? What about plants? A number of researchers are currently involved in studying the claims that plants can sense, or feel, a wide range of emotions. Books and articles in this area are enjoying widespread popularity. Much of the work is flagrantly sensationalistic. Much of it presents unwarranted and premature conclusions. But all of it is intriguing. Plants are, after all, "alive." We certainly do share something very significant with them. If we are inclined to identify life with awareness or consciousness (as we have obviously done with our definition of the soul), then we must come to terms with the plant kingdom.

And as long as we are being so democratic about it all, why not invite the inorganic world into our exclusive club? Scientists and philosophers have occasionally toyed with the notion that crystals may be "alive." They do reproduce themselves. They exert an influence upon their environment and in turn are affected by it. Are viruses alive? There is at least some disagreement here. Where can we say with certainty that there are not even the most primitive and unsophisticated rudiments of life? Cleve Backster, who has done extensive research with things like polygraphs and philodendrons, believes that a basic primal perception can be demonstrated not only in plants, but in such inorganic substances as certain kinds of metals, crystals, and triply distilled water.[3] In his article "On the Symmetry Principle," F. L. Kuntz notes that there is no longer any reasonable doubt that consciousness is a quality which extends throughout the organic realm of living things. But he says further that there are increasing data suggesting that some basic quality of consciousness may even be found "below the threshold of life."[4] This is basically what is claimed by one of the oldest metaphysical positions in philosophy, known as hylozoism. This is, broadly, a doctrine which holds that life is an intrinsic property of all substance, inorganic as well as organic. It is the belief that matter, in all its forms, contains the quality of life. Hylozoism is a metaphysical concept of reality as living substance, and it is not such an unusual doctrine as one might suppose. Thales, traditionally thought of as the first philosopher, was a hylozoist. He shared, with many Egyptian philosophers, the belief that all things are alive. Empedocles also taught that all things in the universe are alive and capable of thought. With roots in the deepest reaches of intellectual antiquity and branches pushing their way into several contemporary disciplines, our suggestion of some quality of unity in opposites is no idle observation.

Many scientists have long believed that there is a kind of symmetry to reality. It is not something they know. It is something they feel. We live in a universe of action and reaction. There are negatively charged particles—electrons—and positively charged particles—protons. If there is matter, then there is antimatter. Speculation about the existence of black holes in the universe feeds speculation about the possibility of white holes, with equally puzzling, but opposite, properties. The assumption of symmetry has not been proved, and it is not even clear just what it entails. But this feeling that reality tends to mirror itself has enabled the mind of man to speculate, sometimes with startling success, in matters of particle theory and cosmology. It is being extended to the very concepts of space and time themselves.

If we may indulge ourselves in a bit of metaphysical speculation (and after all, that is the real fun of philosophy), we might consider the possibility that reality is not only symmetrical but perhaps severely curved. That is to say, the metaphysical structure of reality may be such that whatever exists must be grounded in an ultimate union, thereby making sense out of the notion that apparent opposites trace their source to a point of identity. We have seen some indication of this in political theory (the similarity of the radical left and right), in cosmology (the meeting of the two "ends" of the universe), in biology (the immortal qualities of the amoeba and "God"), in metaphysics and theology (the union of being and nonbeing), even, to further stretch a point, in literature ("It was the best of times; it was the worst of times . . ."). It may be that the most incompatible opposites imaginable are much closer to each other than we have realized. And what of the opposition of life and death? Certainly they make strange bedfellows. Yet there is no question that a complete understanding of either would eliminate all mystery in the other. We can separate them only arbitrarily. Philosophy of death is in fact philosophy of life. The true philosopher is always pursuing death and dying, but only because he is driven to understand life.

We seem, as human beings, to stand somewhere between two opposites. What could be further from us than the lowly amoeba? Perhaps God. God and the amoeba are at least as opposite as life and death. Yet even here we have found some similarity. From our vantage point, which somehow ranges over the entire continuum of the possibilities of consciousness, we can recognize a quality of immortality at either end of the spectrum. Religions in the Oriental tradition claim that the individual is in fact God. The proposition sounds quite blasphemous to the typical Western ear. But we would do well not to dismiss too easily the wisdom of the East. What is meant here is that our individual egos are ultimately grounded in and essentially identical with the absolute, what R. M. Bucke, a Canadian psychiatrist, has called Cosmic Consciousness. Further, these traditions insist that reality is One, the exact position of the ancient Greek philosopher Parmenides. This means that we are not "really" distinct and separated from "other" things. At our very deepest levels we are essentially and intimately interconnected with the reality of all beings. Therefore, even the amoeba is not to be despised. His essence is that of the cosmic One. The ultimate ground of our being is here understood as the ultimate reality of all things. It is no accident that Tillich refers to God interchangeably as the Ground of Being and Being-Itself.

Perhaps at this point we have arrived at the necessity of doing some God-talk.

CHAPTER 5
God-Talk

One of the more satisfying aspects of my theological studies centered around the continuing debates on the various issues in religion. Very immodestly, we would attempt to settle the most intractable questions in theology, from the existence of God to the status of miracles. In all these debates a rather healthy number of seminarians were quite willing to present their ideas and listen with at least strained patience to opposing views. The more important the question, it seemed, the more spirited were the debates. I was therefore quite startled when I found that it was very nearly impossible for me to get a debate going on the question of immortality. I had been growing increasingly skeptical about the possibility of survival beyond the grave and was interested in what those who accepted such a thing had to say. But whenever I broached the subject I found that only others who were skeptical were willing to discuss the issue. For the most part, those who had a strong belief in immortality simply refused to subject their views to the rigors of debate. I was genuinely puzzled. These same persons had no hesitation at all in tackling the myriad questions in theology other than immortality. They were eager to defend such beliefs as the existence of God, the fact of the resurrection, and even such minor matters as the withering of the fig tree under the curse of Jesus. But they tended to clam up when it came to any debate on the question of immortality. Why? "I just don't want to discuss it," said one of my favorite antagonists. Finally, after what must have been obnoxious persistence on my part, he said, "Well, if there isn't any life after death, that's it. I might just as well go out and shoot myself.'' It was difficult, at first, to take him seriously. It struck me that, if this life is all that I have, the one thing I certainly would *not* want to do is hasten my death. Yet he was at the very least giving a clear signal of just how important his belief in immortality was to him. It transcended even his belief in God, which he held strongly but never hesitated to defend.

Bertrand Russell, in his well-known essay ''Why I am not a Christian,'' defines a Christian as one who believes in God, accepts Jesus as at least the best and wisest of men, and believes in personal immortality. Of course most Christians believe far more than these three specific elements of doctrine, but Russell is claiming that these represent the main beliefs of all Christians, whether liberal or conservative. Russell, when writing this essay, had not considered the possibility of being a Christian atheist, a position developed much later in the Death-of-God theologies. But in my first reading of his essay I had little quarrel with his first two points. I was not sure about the third. It was not then clear to me that the most important three beliefs of a Christian would include an acceptance of immortality. Having now encountered a surprising reluctance on the part of my colleagues to discuss immortality, I was beginning to change my mind. In fact it now seems obvious that, for many people, a belief in immortality is even more important than their belief in God or Jesus.

A strong case can be made for the idea that many Christians believe in God and Christ because such beliefs help guarantee their primary desire for immortality. It is often said that God is to be worshiped ''for his own sake, not for what he can do for you.'' But that is pure nonsense. If there is nothing God can do for me, then it is difficult to understand just how I could possibly have any motivation toward worshiping him. The importance of

God is that he can guarantee my survival beyond the grave. The significance of Christ is, for most Christians, his demonstration of immortality in the resurrection. Although it may not be recognized, those who accept a religious position often do so because of a primary desire for immortality. In such cases belief in God stems, at least in part, from a wish for eternal life. Belief in immortality is not generally based on a prior belief in God. This analysis involves a radical adjustment in the priorities of most Christians because it is not widely recognized. The belief in God is simply not the most important belief they have. The real motive is nearly always the more personal one of survival. Suppose, for example, that it could be demonstrated that God does indeed exist, but we do *not* survive the grave. It is a possibility not often considered by Christians. It thrusts right at the heart of why one believes in God.

The belief in God is not always inseparable from a belief in immortality, and perhaps the best example of this comes from the history of the Old Testament. The earlier writings are quite lacking in any belief in survival of the grave. It is not until the much later works—for example, the book of Daniel—that a concept of immortality is developed. God's great promise to Abraham was not immortality, but rather the prosperity of his descendants. There is no indication that Moses expected anything beyond a survival in the memory of his people. Moses was a prophet "whom the Lord knew face to face" (Deut. 34:10b), and yet his greatest blessing was a glimpse of the promised land before he died. The covenant he created between the Hebrew people and their God carried no promise of immortality, but rather one of prosperity and success in this world so long as the vows were kept. Qoheleth, the preacher of Ecclesiastes, writes: "For the fate of the sons of men and the fate of beasts is the same; as one dies, so dies the other. They all have the same breath, and man has no advantage over the beasts;

for all is vanity. All go to one place; all are from the dust, and all turn to dust again'' (Eccl. 3:19-20). If the living have any advantage over the dead it is only in this: ''For the living know that they will die, but the dead know nothing, and they have no more reward'' (Eccl. 9:5*a*). It is obviously possible for a people to have a strong belief in and commitment to their God without a corresponding belief in immortality.

But it is unusual. Especially in the Christian tradition, the belief in God cannot be understood apart from the desire to achieve eternal life. For this reason any philosophy of death must include a chapter dealing with the concept of God. We must begin to understand the importance of a belief in God and the implications of that belief for the possibilities of immortality.

For some people, talk of God is an intellectual embarrassment. Their belief in God has gone the way of Santa Claus and the Easter Bunny. They are as unable to bring themselves to speak seriously of God as they are of elves and fairies. For others, God-talk is just what they do most easily and most often, sometimes because their concept of God has not gone beyond Santa Claus and the Easter Bunny. Still others believe that God-talk is to be avoided. They are strongly convinced that no one has the slightest idea what he is talking about when he speaks of God. No two people seem to mean the same thing when they use the word ''God.'' To a large extent this feeling is an accurate one. The concept of God produces wildly different images in people. It follows that the affirmation ''I believe in God'' may not mean the same thing when two people make it. But if this is true, it would seem that the claim ''I do not believe in God'' can be just as ambiguous. A student once came to me and announced defiantly, ''I don't believe in God.'' My clever response was immediate interest and an invitation to ''sit right down and tell me what kind of God you don't believe in, and I will tell you what kind of God I don't believe in.''

There is, to be sure, a lot of confusion at this point. It seems absolutely impossible for us to determine whether God exists or not, or even to come to some sort of agreement on just what the word "God" means. With this in mind, some have suggested that we declare a sort of moratorium on the use of the word "God." Perhaps we should simply put it on the shelf and get on to other, more substantial, things. But if we have any interest in developing a philosophy of death, we cannot take this suggestion seriously. We have seen that the concept is just too important for us to ignore in our contemplation of the meaning of death. Any total consideration of death must come to grips with the idea of God.

In fact it is possible to develop a reasonable definition of God that will avoid the most serious problems of God-talk and provide us with what we need. We can define God in such a way as to eliminate the relevance of all arguments concerning his existence. And we can do so with a definition that should be acceptable to most people who believe in God. It is a very large order, but there is no difficulty here because the major work has already been done. Paul Tillich has laid the groundwork for us in his definition of God as Being-Itself. Tillich is saying that God, whoever or whatever he is, must certainly be the source, or ground, of reality. Tillich sometimes refers to God as the ground of being. These references to God imply the presence of a reality beyond the *things* of reality. Tillich considers God to be not a thing, or a being, but rather a metaphysical reality in which all things and beings are somehow grounded. But this suggests that God is an abstraction underlying the world of concrete things, and such a concept is not compatible with traditional theology. I suggest that we adjust our Tillichian terminology a bit and define God as Ultimate Reality. We gain some definite advantages with such a definition. If we can understand God as Ultimate Reality, then it is clearly pointless for us to spend any time arguing about whether God exists. Certainly Ultimate Reality, whatever it is, *is*. Even if one rejects the implication that there may be degrees of reality, it is difficult to deny that there must be an ultimate nature, or source, or ground of reality. Whatever it is that serves as the ground of being simply cannot fail to be, although Tillich explicitly denies that the ground of being can be said to "exist" in the same way objects exist. Ultimate Reality is whatever you find when you have gone as far as possible into the nature of existence itself. It is the Necessary Being, required by the ontological argument for the existence of God. It is the final, all-inclusive explanation of reality postulated by the cosmological argument—the Aristotelian Unmoved Mover. It is the first cause in which all subsequent effects are grounded. We do not know whether Ultimate Reality is the God of Abraham, Isaac, and Jacob, or whether it is Brahman or Cosmic Consciousness. It may be the subatomic forces within the atom, or the Big Bang, or perhaps some primordial cosmic quark. It may be something utterly unknown. But Ultimate Reality is surely real.

Further, the definition of God as Ultimate Reality should be quite acceptable to anyone who believes in God. The theologian would not wish to maintain that God is unreal. God is therefore some form, or mode, of reality. It would not be a reasonable position to suppose that God is anything less than Ultimate Reality. And God cannot be more than Ultimate Reality since, by definition, there can be nothing more ultimate than Ultimate Reality.

The definition obviously has a watered-down quality to it in that we still do not have any idea as to the *nature* of Ultimate Reality. We have taken a necessary first step in understanding God as the heart of being, the very ground of is-ness. But the definition of God as Ultimate Reality hardly solves all the problems in theology, or even the most important ones. We do

75

not know whether Ultimate Reality is a personal being, or whether Ultimate Reality cares about us or is aware in any sense at all. But at least we can avoid the distractions of all those fascinating, but highly frustrating, arguments for and against the existence of God. Any debate over whether God exists would, on this definition, be somewhat similar to a discussion of whether is-ness is. There is still much work to be done. But this definition is a useful one for our purposes, because we can now begin to consider the nature of Ultimate Reality and understand its implications for a philosophy of death.

There are those who would consider the cozy relationship between God and death to be unfortunate. Their thinking would be that it should be possible to make an intelligent, reasoned study of death without having to deal with certain extraneous elements in theology like the question of God. The feeling is that such considerations can only bog us down, distract us from the real issues of death. This is not necessarily a denial of the importance of other questions in philosophy and theology, but rather a feeling of "let's take 'em on one at a time." Yet we have seen that this may not be possible here. Our beliefs about death are simply too colored by our beliefs about God. Whether a person believes in God or not often dictates his attitudes toward death. Or perhaps, as suggested earlier, whether a person desires immortality or not dictates his attitudes toward God. In any case, our present topic necessarily involves us in a consideration of the concept of God.

We have suggested that the definition of God as Ultimate Reality be accepted as a sufficient starting point for our purposes. We can avoid the time-consuming arguments concerning the existence of God and begin a consideration of the nature of Ultimate Reality. After presenting, in broad outline, the possible modes that Ultimate Reality might take, I will argue that this may open up a curiously neglected area of study—an area that might yield some useful data for our inquiry.

The law of excluded middle allows us to assume that, whatever the nature of Ultimate Reality might be, it is either some form of awareness or it is not. Further, the ontological status of Ultimate Reality will tend toward either the abstract, as Tillich suggests, or the concrete. We are assuming that Ultimate Reality *is* in some sense. Just *what* it is presents difficulties. But it is not hard to outline the major options.

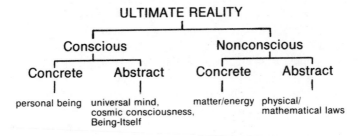

The basic distinction is clearly whether Ultimate Reality is conscious or not. The Judeo-Christian tradition is grounded in the belief that Ultimate Reality (God) is conscious. He is aware. He can, and does, listen to our prayers and make decisions which affect our lives. Our Western heritage presents us with a God understood as a conscious, personal being. This concept of God commits us to the belief that Ultimate Reality is a conscious, concrete (that is, particularized) entity. On this side of the line, God is inevitably anthropomorphic. He is understood as a being differing from us more in quantity than in quality. He

77

is more powerful than we are; in fact he is omnipotent. He is more intelligent—omniscient. He is larger—omnipresent—and, of course, better—omnibenevolent. He is us, raised to an ultimate power by a factor of infinity. He exceeds us in all admirable and worthy respects. He can whip Bobby Fischer in chess, or Wilt Chamberlain in arm-wrestling. He is a superior debater: Job, for example, insists that God could win any argument, even against one whose cause is just (Job 9:13-20). God is to a greater or lesser degree like us, if we accept the idea that Ultimate Reality is to be found in a personal being. The anthropomorphic quality can vary considerably. We find a broad range within the very first book of the Bible. In the third chapter of Genesis God is pictured as "walking in the garden in the cool of the day," like a well-to-do Mesopotamian. Adam and Eve actually hear the sound of his footsteps and even hide from him. This represents a highly anthropomorphic concept of God. The later writings of the first chapter indicate that considerable sophistication in this area has occurred. God no longer is required to walk. His spirit moves over the face of the deep. He still moves in time, makes decisions, and pronounces his work "good." If God is understood as a personal being, a certain anthropomorphic quality is unavoidable. But there is still a wide range of options.

Theologians are sometimes fond of speaking of God as "personal, but not a person." This suggests a more abstract concept of God than that which considers him as a separate, independently existing being, distinct from his creation. There is a definite strain of mysticism here. The understanding of God as the ground of being or even as universal mind or cosmic consciousness proceeds from a sense that Ultimate Reality is not to be found in anything concrete or particularized. Being-Itself may somehow serve as the substratum of all beings, but it cannot stand as one (bigger) being among others. Mystics have long insisted that God is not an object, but rather that by which we understand the ultimate oneness of all objects. Ultimate Reality is more of a quality than an entity. No being, however superior to other beings, seems adequate as the final ground for reality. Ultimate Reality, on this analysis, is mental rather than physical. The notion of mind is already more abstract than the usual concepts of physical substance, and Cosmic Mind carries this tendency to its ultimate conclusions. God, as awareness, may not be conscious of things in the way we are. There may be, for example, no subject-object distinction in the awareness of God. But if we can begin to work with the concept of awareness-as-such, we may be closer to an understanding of God.

On the other side, it is entirely possible that Ultimate Reality neither is nor has awareness. This is the position that most people who deny the existence of God would take, although our definition of God as Ultimate Reality makes them believers of a sort. Some have argued that any definition of God which makes it impossible for a person to be an atheist must be meaningless. We cannot ignore the very real differences between the believer and the nonbeliever, and it is simply ridiculous to conjure up a definition which does this. But our definition does not avoid the obvious distinctions between the theist and the atheist. It is entirely consistent for one to accept the definition of God as Ultimate Reality and yet profess atheism. Technically, an atheist is one who denies theism. But theism is a very specific position. It does not even begin to include all beliefs in God. The theist God is the God of traditional Judaism and Christianity. It is the belief that God is a personal being. All other options are literally atheistic, that is, they are denials of the theistic view of Ultimate Reality. We have not defined atheism out of existence with our equation of God with Ultimate Reality. We have only insisted that there is no reasonable way one can doubt the reality of Ultimate Reality. All of us, whether theists or not, are seeking the metaphysical keys by which reality can be understood. Those who hold that Ultimate Reality is the matter/energy synthesis of the physical world will understandably be reluctant to refer to this as God, and they are certainly entitled to avoid using the word. They are still atheists. But in our common pursuit of truth we are all believers, for whatever that is worth.

The belief that Ultimate Reality is nonconscious need not take the position of nineteenth-century Newtonian physics. We have already suggested that the naïve materialism so popular during the period immediately preceding the development of Heisenberg's Principle of Uncertainty and Einstein's theories of relativity has been rather thoroughly humbled. The complaint that theology and metaphysics have become too abstract is not an uncommon one, but it applies equally well to science. A God whose footsteps I might hear in the garden is certainly easier to understand than a God who serves as the ground of my being. But a universe composed of hard little atomic marbles is far easier to grasp than one containing quarks, anti-matter, neutrinos, and tachyons. The ability to do abstract thinking is an absolute prerequisite for anyone who might wish even an elementary understanding of Ultimate Reality as seen by today's scientists. The mind-bending advancements in the areas of particle theory, quantum mechanics, and astronomy suggest that the final truths about reality will be quite inconsistent with the concrete view of the universe as a celestial pool table. Ultimate Reality may better be understood as the puzzling operations of certain basic and necessary principles, granting to abstractions the final source of creation as we know it. Whatever the final answers are, they promise to be conceptually startling. A student of mine once said to me, "If I knew 'The Truth,' I could explain it to you in fifteen minutes." I think I know what he was trying to say, but I doubt that he is correct.

CHAPTER 6
Philosophy, Science, and Death

Whatever "The Truth" turns out to be, it has interesting implications for any philosophy of death. We know that we are. We do not know from whence we came. We are equally ignorant of our final destiny. But one thing is certain. We came from someplace, or more accurately, we were created from something. Philosophy of death is concerned in part with where we are going, or to what we will return. Our final destiny is directly related to the nature of Ultimate Reality. If Ultimate Reality is identical with the God of Abraham, Isaac, and Jacob, then it is reasonable to believe that our death will bring a reunion with our creator. If Ultimate Reality has the quality of the mystic's cosmic soul, then we should expect finally to merge into that substance. If the materialists have been right all along, then our destiny is one of a disintegration of our physical substance into its separate components. If Ultimate Reality is the more abstract workings of basic physical and mathematical laws, then we ourselves are essentially the product of such laws and can anticipate a final reconciliation with them.

Whatever Ultimate Reality is, it is the meeting point of life and death. Whatever it was that gave us our being holds the key to what happens to us after death. We exist as sentient beings, ignorant both of our source and our destiny, but convinced that there are explanations, and that we will one day discover them. Presumably at death we are reunited with the ground of our being. We cannot escape from what we essentially are. We must inevitably return to the ultimate source out of which we have come. The suggestion here is that our existential status after death should be quite similar to our existential status prior to conception. We will eventually be returned to what we once were. The assumption that our metaphysical status after death is similar to, or identical with, our situation prior to our conception is difficult to prove. But it seems to make a basic sort of sense. Ultimate Reality, however it is understood, is our creator and our final destiny. It is our beginning and our end, or theologically our Alpha and our Omega. It has spawned us and is continuously drawing us back into itself. It has given us life and will reabsorb us in death. Proper humility forces me to confess that it may not be so. Our eternal destiny may be radically different from anything we have ever been. We may have been created out of nothing, to endure an eternity of being. We may somehow have come from Ultimate Reality, never to return to that status.

But if we are returned in death to the very ground of our being, then we are beginning to unravel another thread in the metaphysical knot called "death." Because if this analysis is true, then it promises some very exciting things. We can understand our present existence as an interlude between two more basic compositions. The fear of death may be partially eased. We are not frightened of what the Zen master referred to as "the shape of our face before we were born." We should then not fear the shape of our face after death. We have been there before. It provides at least a vague hope that whatever it was that created us once could do it again. Whatever Ultimate Reality is, it once upon a time resulted in us. There is no good reason to suppose that it could not happen again. But far more important, the notion that the other side of the grave may be similar to the other side of birth opens up the possibility of new ways of studying death. We may actually be able to resolve some of the questions raised by a philosophy of death.

We have noted that the study of death is attended by some very serious problems, not the least of which is the fact that death appears to remove us from being able to study at all. As soon as we are in a position to know what it is all about (i.e., when we are actually dead), it would seem that we are in a status such that it is impossible to know anything at all, including what death is all about. This is a very real problem and, if we ignore for the moment the possibility of communication with the dead, it would appear to be insurmountable. We can deal with the living, but we can only look at the dead. We are prevented from understanding them. We simply cannot peek through the film of the present to the incoming future. But perhaps we are focusing our efforts in the wrong direction. We can look into the past. If our ultimate future is like our ultimate past, then perhaps we can learn something of death from the past. We can only guess at the future. But we do have access to the past. There are no records of what is to come. But what has been is never lost.

How can we explore our past? The past we are talking about seems hidden by a veil at least as opaque as that surrounding the future. We are talking about examining our pre-uterine history, and we have no memories or records of that. Yet there are tools at our disposal. Philosophy of death has ignored the potentials of hypnosis and in-depth psychoanalysis. Sigmund Freud, a pioneer in the study of hypnosis, believed strongly that a deep trance state is a legitimate means of exploring areas of memory not otherwise accessible. Freudian psychoanalysts even believe that they have discovered genuine memories traceable to the womb. This is correctly held to be of monumental importance to psychology. But as C. G. Jung has noted, neither Freud nor his followers made the attempt to go back further than the womb.[1] It apparently never occurred to Freud to probe even deeper into the memory patterns beyond the moment of conception. For our purposes this would have been of far greater significance because he would have been dealing with the very heart of our interests here. Freud would have been penetrating into the mysteries of death.

Why did he not do it? Even the remotest promise of resolving the metaphysical questions of death should have been enough to justify the attempt. Jung suggests that Freud never pursued this line of research simply because his basic presuppositions prevented it. The materialistic, naturalistic assumptions held by Freud precluded his making any efforts to go past the point of conception. The moment of conception was Freud's cul-de-sac. It literally never occurred to Freud that memories from the womb might not be the earliest memories that we have. Freud bracketed his own research with his presuppositions. In this he was no different from any of us. We all tend to confine our inquiries to the realm of the possible. But we often forget that we define the possible, or at least our understanding of it. When asked how he ever conceived of his special and general theories of relativity, Einstein is said to have remarked that his most creative speculations did not occur until he first realized that even axioms could be doubted. Once he began questioning some of the most basic assumptions of physics he found new vistas opening up to him. But even Einstein had his brackets. He went to his grave believing that "God does not play dice with the universe." This was his way of insisting that, contrary to the rapidly increasing body of data suggesting otherwise, an inflexible chain of cause and effect determines the shapes of reality.

Suppose, for a moment, that Freud had questioned his own materialistic axioms. Suppose that he had been willing to entertain at least the possibility of experiences before conception, and therefore could have taken seriously the chance that he might be able to explore them by means of hypnosis. What might he have found? According to Jung, Freud would have found himself sounding out a vast, boundless sea of racial and interracial memories, including some of the most basic experiences of earliest rational man. These would be the archetypes from which we construct our own mental categories. On Jung's analysis, Freud would now be tapping into the "collective unconscious." The Tibetans would expect Freud to have delved into a period of bizarre mental experiences on the Bardo plane preceded by another existence on the physical plane. They would not stop even with the collective unconscious, but would rather proceed to ever further depths of the remote past which is our own personal history.

At this point it may appear as though we have been assuming some sort of immortality, at least in the direction of the past. We seem to have taken for granted the eternality of the soul, which would allow for the possibility of memories before the moment of conception. It might be said that this procedure we have discussed is valid only with the prior assumption that we "existed" before we were conceived, and this assumption, of course, just may not be true. Most people would insist that it is *probably* not true, and that we would be wasting our time banking on a very marginal concept of metaphysics. But I would claim that this is a valid avenue of exploration regardless of which metaphysical system is accepted. It does not depend upon an assumption that we have had a previous existence, nor does it assume that Freud's presuppositions were wrong. Depending on what the nature of Ultimate Reality is, our original status was either conscious or nonconscious. If science is correct in telling us that nothing is really created or destroyed, then we obviously existed in *some* sense prior to the moment of conception. We may have existed only as a dispersion of the components of matter and energy which later came together to give us our being. But whatever is the case, any suggestions such as have been made here should be large enough to allow for all possibilities.

If Ultimate Reality is some mode of consciousness, then we should be able to learn something of it from a careful use of the techniques of hypnosis and psychoanalysis. But suppose it is not. Ultimate Reality may be a nonmental substratum of consciousness itself, and our primordial union with it would presumably be without memories. If that original, ultimate stuff out of which we came is nonconscious in nature, then of course it would not be possible for us to have experienced it. It would therefore not be possible for us to remember it. What would this imply for our suggestion that the questions of death might be explored at the pre-uterine level? Just this. If, after intensive, serious, and prolonged efforts by trained, capable, and dedicated people, the attempt to probe past the moment of conception is unsuccessful, if no valid evidence is found of any pre-uterine consciousness, this would be strong evidence against the various theories of reincarnation and those metaphysical systems which view Ultimate Reality as some form of cosmic mind. Our attention could then be more precisely focused on the options which are left. Hypnotism and psychoanalysis—they are meager tools, to be sure. There are enormous difficulties in judging the validity of their data. We know that the hypnotic subject is highly suggestible when in a trance state. While he is unlikely to lie, there is a strong tendency to please the hypnotist who controls the trance. The suggestion that hypnotism can be useful in studying the possibility of previous experience is not new. What might be called "the Bridey Murphey syndrome" has occasioned moments of excitement before, usually with disappointing results. But the possibility that research in this area may have important implications for our understanding of death has certainly not been emphasized. The methods of hypnosis and psychoanalysis are notorious for their deceptions, but are even more remarkable for their successes. They just might be useful in helping us to construct a reasonable philosophy of death.

There are other ways, even more promising, in which science and philosophy might pool their efforts in this area. The significance of parapsychological research in an understanding of death has not received the attention it deserves. We may be on the threshold of some major breakthroughs of knowledge which will ripple their way through the stagnant waters of every intellectual discipline. The biggest step is being taken now. It involves the status of parapsychological studies themselves. Legitimate research into parapsychological phenomona has long been hindered by accusations of anti-scientific occultism. To a large extent this may have been a valid criticism during the early stages, and certainly carries some weight even today. The field of parapsychology has always tended to draw a strange crowd. Its devotees have included a disproportionate number of the superstitious, the gullible, and out-and-out charlatans. They accused science of being narrow-minded, sterile, and pedantic. But they were themselves guilty of an anti-intellectual bias against rational, structured, controlled inquiry. The situation appears to be quite different today. Arthur Koestler has pointed to an apparent reversal in the traditional positions of physics and parapsychology, noting that laboratories devoted to the study of E.S.P. and the like have settled into the rather dry routine of standard, controlled experiments and lengthy statistics tables, while science grapples with such "occult" concepts as time inversion and multidimensional spaces.[2] Koestler further observes that the British Society for Psychical Research includes among its past presidents "three Nobel laureates, ten Fellows of the Royal Society, one Prime Minister and a galaxy of professors, mostly physicists and philosophers."[3] That the data of parapsychology are being taken seriously by some of the cream of intelligentsia simply cannot be denied.

There are basically two ways in which parapsychology might help answer our questions pertaining to death. One has to do with the possible explanations of the data of parapsychology, the other with a very specific area of parapsychological research. In the light of what we now know about the possibilities of E.S.P., it would be quite dogmatic for anyone simply to deny that there is anything to it. The evidence for E.S.P. is too great for us to dismiss it as entirely the result of fraud or ignorance. But having accepted the notion that extrasensory perception might be genuine, how are we to understand it? What possible explanations are available? It has often been assumed that any acceptance of E.S.P. would be a strong prima facie case for the independence of mind and body. E.S.P., if it exists at all, would surely be an example of an interconnectedness on the mental level—that is, evidence of mind "touching" mind. Since it is clear that such examples do not involve brain touching brain, what other explanations would be likely? On this analysis, any acceptance of E.S.P. would yield the inescapable conclusion that the mind is after all an independent substance not necessarily limited to the spatial and temporal coordinates of the brain. But this line of reasoning may not be valid. In fact it is not difficult to construct theories which might account for most examples of E.S.P. without providing any evidence for the independent existence of mind. Such theories can be based upon the assumption that the brain, when properly understood, will finally provide the explanations on a physical level without the need for any hypothesis giving the mind an independent existential status. The brain, for example, is clearly some sort of electrochemical radio-computer. It can receive or transmit signals via the medium of electrical charges as expressed in neural impulses throughout the body. Perhaps it can also transmit or receive through a process of electro-radiation across distances to or from other objects or brains. If so, we have no need to resort to speculations beyond the physical mode in order to explain the possibility of extrasensory perception. The reality of E.S.P. may not entail the independent existence of the mind.

Well, it really does not matter. Perhaps the final explanation of E.S.P. will support the independent existence of the mind. Perhaps it will not. While we might harbor some hopes one way or another, our real interest is in the discovery of *the* answer, even if it is not our answer. However E.S.P. is explained, it will have implications for our study of death, since any increase in our understanding of the mind cannot fail to provide further material for us to work with in our attempts to understand death. It continues to be a basic thesis of this book that the metaphysical explanation of death cannot be resolved without a corresponding explanation of mental processes. We do not know what death is simply because we do not know what the mind is. We are puzzled about what happens to the mind at death because we do not yet understand our mental experience of life.

I sometimes ask my students what they would choose if some little green gremlin (neither the color nor the species is important) offered them total understanding either of life or of death. Which area of knowledge would be most important to them? Most people have little trouble deciding upon one or the other, but as they defend their decisions something very interesting happens. A student who chooses, say, life, begins to see that the reasons behind his choice are basically identical with those of his colleague who has chosen to understand death. It has to do ultimately with the desire to "know thyself." The point is that it really makes very little difference which choice is made. The final result is an understanding of the self. Only the direction chosen to reach that understanding is different.

The assumption that research into the realms of E.S.P. can

provide data for our philosophical interest in life and death rests upon the notion that life and mind are two ways of talking about the same thing. Teilhard de Chardin has made a persuasive case for the idea that the prime characteristic of life is awareness. All living things exhibit this quality to some degree and in some mode. It is certainly not too much to suggest that the matrix of awareness is something which might be called mental substance. Whether such substance is a modification of physical substance is not known. But an explanation of the dynamics of E.S.P. cannot fail to provide significant insights into the workings of the mind. An understanding of the mind is virtually the equivalent of an understanding of life. That a complete understanding of life would resolve the mysteries of death seems obvious. It is almost too neat to be believed, but it is this analysis which supports the contention that a comprehensive study of E.S.P. must eventually yield valuable information for a philosophy of death. It should be remembered that the philosopher, like the scientist, is driven not simply to prove his presuppositions, but rather to discover the truth. E.S.P. may or may not lend support to a given metaphysical theory, but it should not be ignored. Any data that can be provided by research into the realms of parapsychology should be welcomed by anyone who seeks the truth about death.

There is an area of parapsychology which deals more specifically with the question of death. It has to do with the activities of spiritualists or mediums who claim to be able to contact and receive information from the dead. My own intellectual, logical, and cultural parameters force me to present this field very hesitantly. There is no great difficulty in accepting other manifestations of E.S.P. as areas to be taken seriously. But communication with the dead? It seems hard to believe that this could possibly have a scientific basis. The "sittings" take place in surroundings hardly calculated to encourage an objective appraisal. They are generally attended by those who have a strong prior disposition to accept the validity of contact with the dead. The lighting is usually subdued. The participants are required to remain seated and relatively motionless. The opportunities for snooping about are minimal. It can be admitted that there are a number of rather startling accounts which claim to be cases of communication beyond the grave. But we cannot now be sure of the correct explanations.

One of the more serious difficulties in the area of spirit contact stems from the possibility that such occasions might be accounted for by genuine extrasensory perceptions rather than spirits. In those instances, for example, where a medium provides information which is apparently unknown to him, it may be that the medium has tapped into the mental apparatus of the living rather than the dead. It may be "only" a case of mind-reading and not communication with the dead. In at least one instance, two women prepared for a seance by reading a novel and picking one of the fictitious characters as their deceased relative. They talked about him and thought about him until they felt that they knew him. Then they went to a spiritualist to seek information from their imaginary kin. The spiritualist proceeded to describe the man and give the women messages from him. The accuracy of the description was impressive, the messages appropriate to the character involved. The one difficulty was simply that the man had never existed except from the pen of some author and as a concept in the mind of the two women. There are a number of possible explanations here, but one of them has to be the chance that some spiritualists are not out-and-out frauds, but rather gifted people who do not quite understand their own talents. Perhaps they can pick up information from other minds and they attribute it to the wrong source. But then there are other stories which purport to be cases in which the medium provides valid information which could not possibly be known by anyone alive. It is a curious area, indeed.

But there is another objection to the phenomena of spirit-communication which might be considered far more serious. One would reasonably expect that contact with the dead should provide, not just interesting, but genuinely startling information of a depth and profundity unmatched in any other area. Those who have died and yet somehow survived must certainly have made the most significant metaphysical dis-coveries imaginable. They do not merely believe in immortality. That option is available on this side of the grave. They *know* that immortality is a fact. They know it because they are experiencing it as a reality present to their immediate awareness. They have died and yet they live on. But even more than that, they know far more than the fact of immortality. They know the *mode* of immortality. In other words, they are experiencing not simply the objective reality of immortality, but also its subjective qualities. They know the shape of consciousness after death. They should be expected to have a metaphysical knowledge not available to us. They would have a perspective on reality spanning both sides of the grave. Their expanded knowledge would, in comparison to our own, be godlike. Their relationship to us would be at least that of the one-eyed man in the land of the blind. Imagine what they could teach us! They might not have all the answers, but surely they should have some of the more interesting ones. It is not too much to expect that the quality of their knowledge, while perhaps less than absolute, should nevertheless vastly exceed our own. Superior qualities of wisdom and metaphysical insight into the nature of things should be a mark of any valid communication with the dead. But it is precisely in these respects that we are most disappointed. Such information as is conveyed through "spirit-communication" is nearly always philosophically shallow, even silly. At best, it seems no better than what might be obtained or guessed at without the advantage of communication with the dead. At worst, it is simply intellectually embarrassing. Seances seem generally to provide *reductio ad absurdum* arguments against their own validity. A. E. Taylor speaks of the "intellectual and moral idiocy" of such revelations, suggesting that the kindest interpretation of such phenomena would be to suppose that, "if they are what they claim to be, we can only hope that the unseen world, like the seen, has its homes for the feebleminded, and that it is with their inmates that our occultists are in communication." [4]

It would be unseemly for us to jump to any premature conclusions in the area of parapsychology. There are serious difficulties which have not entirely been overcome. Science demands the quality of repeatability in its experiments before any information from them can be accepted as genuine. But the hit-and-miss aspect of parapsychology hinders its acceptance by the scientific community. Sometimes it works, and sometimes it does not. Of course this might easily be accounted for by insisting that we have not developed our talents and powers in this area to the point where they are entirely under our control. To some extent this is certainly true. The landscape of our own minds is not as well understood as the topography of the moon. But the data from parapsychology may lend themselves to explanations less esoteric than the supposition of mysterious nonphysical powers in the mind. There is the ever-present possibility of fraud. Many of the abilities demonstrated by subjects in E.S.P. research can be duplicated by magicians and sleight-of-hand artists. Several times such subjects have been caught in an outright deception. Their talents often have an embarrassing tendency to wane in the presence of capable magicians who understand the dynamics of deception.

What is the most reasonable position to take regarding

parapsychology? We can be sure that the data are not to be explained within the boundaries of reality as Newton defined it. Reality does not appear to be what Newtonian physics once thought it was. To some extent such phenomena accommodate themselves to quite "naturalistic" explanations, including coincidence, nonverbal cues, and fraud. But only the most unscientific mind will dismiss *a priori* all "paranormal" events as variations on a materialistic theme of metaphysics. The world of the scientist and of the philosopher has become too awesomely large, both spatially and conceptually, for us to suppose that we have the keys to understanding it. There are far too many doors we do not even know about.

We cannot be content to leave the impression that science is relevant to the study of death only in the rather marginal areas of hypnosis, psychotherapy, and parapsychology. There are, in fact, a number of other possible ways in which the mysteries of death might be opened up in the laboratory. But they are all predicated upon the assumption that science can and should devote itself to a study of the mind. We should remember that death is a philosophical problem insofar as it relates to the processes of consciousness. From this it seems to follow that an understanding of the dynamics of mind ought to yield an understanding of the metaphysics of death. In other words, to the extent that the mind becomes a legitimate object of scientific study, science promises to be of significant value in the resolution of what is now a philosophical issue. But science must study the structure and substance of consciousness. Such a statement seems so obvious as to be trivial. But it bears closer examination.

There are several considerations which have led some to argue that the mind is not a legitimate entity for the scientist to study. These fall basically into two categories, both of which were advanced in a dialogue I once had with a behavorial psychologist. His first point was that the mind, understood as something distinct from brain processes, is not a legitimate object for scientific analysis simply because it is not a legitimate object at all. The assumption here is that stubbornly persistent billiard-ball cosmology, or to mix my metaphors, the dragon of materialism which refuses to be slain. Against this argument I boldly conceded—and proceeded. I must acknowledge that consciousness is not an object in the usual sense of that term. But the usual sense of that term is materialistic. I continue to deny that, because consciousness fails to manifest itself as extended substance, it therefore does not exist. Of course it exists. I know that there is mind so long as I myself have subjective experiences (which, alas, is something like saying I know that there is mind so long as I know that there is mind, but that is just about what it amounts to). The strength of Descartes' very simple and very basic argument for the reality of the mind is inescapable. No glib attempt to equate the mind with "electricity" (the definition offered by my behaviorist colleague) or some vaguely defined internal biolumenescence, as suggested by anthropologist Roger W. Wescott, can be accepted as final. The derrière of a glowworm is simply not an adequate analogue of mind. It would certainly be premature to deny that electricity or cellular radiation is involved in the phenomenon of consciousness. Such processes may even be essential, the *sine qua non* of mind. But they are not, as understood now, identical with mind. Subjective experience continues to demand explanation. Sir Julian Huxley, a man certainly without biases toward the occult, easily acknowledged that "our knowledge of physics and chemistry, physiology and neurology does not account for the basic fact of subjective experience." Billiard-ball cosmology is too simplistic to handle the data of consciousness. Huxley notes that "the stark fact of mind sticks in the throat of pure rationalism and reductionist materialism."

The second point made during the course of our dialogue by my behaviorist friend was that, even if he were to consider the suggestion that consciousness is *some*thing having some explanation, he would continue to deny that such explanations could ever be scientific. Therefore, he said, the efforts of science to study the mind are in vain. His concept of science as a discipline seemed limited to his narrow understanding of metaphysics. Nevertheless, this second objection raised against the possibility of science studying the mind presents a legitimate question. Even if he were to acknowledge that consciousness might be some strange thing in some strange sense, he was now asking quite simply how such an "entity" could ever be the proper object of scientific study. Science jealously guards its separation from the occult, and correctly so. We cannot allow ourselves to suggest for a moment that science abandon its objectivity and ignore its own demand for rational explanation. There is abundant evidence that science can research the data of hypnosis and parapsychology without losing anything essential. But even if these are not pursued, there are other, perhaps less threatening, areas in which science might provide the philosopher of death with relevant data.

While denying the identity of brain and mind as physical substance, we realize it is nevertheless obvious that there is some relationship between the two. Let us suppose that we are justified in dismissing the various metaphysics of coincidence which would deny the connection of mind and body. Systems such as Leibniz' theories of parallelism or preestablished harmony, or Malebranche's occasionalism, which affirm the separate existential status of mind and body while denying any connection between the two, place too great a strain on our efforts to be rational. The mind-body problem requires an explanation beyond coincidence or the constant miraculous intervention of divine power. The major options would appear to be: (1) some form of Cartesian dualistic interaction—that is, a belief in the mind and body as distinct entities which somehow do affect each other (although probably not via the pineal gland as Descartes suggested); (2) a variation of Spinoza's double-aspect theory in which the mind and body are understood as modifications of an even more basic substance which is neither mental nor physical; (3) Thomas Henry Huxley's proposal that the mind is a shadowy "epiphenomenon" of the brain, affected by brain processes but exerting no influence in return; or (4) possibly even a metaphysical idealism similar to that suggested by Berkeley in which the mind is understood as the basic reality and physical bodies are either illusory or somehow grounded in the mental.

In any case, the point here is that, while denying the identity of mind and brain (as material substances), we are certainly prepared to acknowledge some kind of very close relationship between them. This means that science, in the very traditional sense, is already able to study the mind, at least indirectly. Science is clearly capable of studying the brain. The recent interest in the area of brain instrumentation, or biofeedback, is an important development. It is a sign of the times that a popular mail-order catalogue now offers an alpha-wave monitor among its many listings. All learning requires some kind of feedback. If we are to learn more about the most important organ in our body such instruments will prove to be invaluable. Sophisticated variations of the electroencephalogram have already disclosed much about the electrical activities of the brain. But even more important, much has been learned about the surprising abilities of the "self" to monitor and regulate a wide range of supposedly autonomic bodily functions. We need not commit ourselves to the enthusiastic claims of instant electronic satori in order to recognize the significance of biofeedback. But research is being done in exploring the relationship between biofeedback and

97

meditation. This could be very significant for a philosophy of death. There is some indication that meditation can produce deathlike experiences. Mystics have long spoken of the concept of ego death in the transcendent experience of cosmic consciousness. The claim is that a genuine ego death can be experienced apart from biological death. A careful study of brain processes during such experiences may be helpful in coming to a more adequate understanding of death. At any rate, it seems clear that any increase in our knowledge about the brain should have implications about how we can understand the mind. And it is, after all, the mind which contains the mysteries of death.

One of the most obvious ways in which death can be studied is to direct our attention to those who are dying and those who have experienced a moment in which they were certain that death was imminent. Such people might be in a position to provide us with some insights into the nature of death. Dr. Russell Noyes, an associate professor of psychiatry at the University of Iowa College of Medicine, believes that his research into the accounts provided by people who have nearly drowned or fallen from great heights or otherwise confronted death directly points toward a common pattern, an identifiable sequence of experiences with some transcendent qualities similar to mystical experiences. He identifies three phases which he refers to as "resistance," "life review," and "transcendence." [5] Several other researchers have noted much the same thing. Dr. Elisabeth Kübler-Ross, in her popular book, *On Death and Dying*, [6] presents the results of many years of working with dying patients. She has identified five distinct stages that dying patients often go through from the moment they first learn that their illness is terminal until the event of death itself. The time required to work through these stages varies considerably, and they do not always follow each other in the standard sequence. Sometimes a stage is skipped over and returned to later.

Sometimes there is a regression to an earlier stage. But in general these five stages seem to be common events in the experience of the dying patient. Dr. Kübler-Ross specifies them as (1) denial and isolation, (2) anger, (3) bargaining, (4) depression, (5) acceptance. Dr. J. Y. Dayananda, chairman of the department of English and Philosophy at Lock Haven State College, has written an interesting article in which he carefully traces the stages delineated by Dr. Kübler-Ross, correlating them with a classic literary treatment of death, Tolstoy's *Death of Ivan Ilych*. In his words, "Dr. Ross' discoveries in her consulting room corroborate Tolstoy's literary insights into the experience of dying." [7] Such treatments, spanning interdisciplinary studies, provide a richer, fuller understanding of the dynamics of death. No adequate development of a philosophy of death is possible if these approaches are neglected.

There are other avenues which might be taken by science and philosophy today that should prove useful in the study of mind and death. Some of these are not obviously relevant and their implications are therefore ignored. But straightforward, hard-nosed research on the submicroscopic level could provide insights into the metaphysics of death. Perhaps, as some have suggested, there is even the possibility of encountering the ultimate constituents or substance of consciousness itself. Arthur Koestler has pointed to what might be a resurrection of the Cartesian notion of mental substance in the speculations of V. A. Firsoff and Sir Cyril Burt. They speculate on the possibility of discovering "mindons," or "psychons," which could be little bits of mind-stuff. [8] Such speculations stir a deep feeling among many philosophers that we are indulging in a category mistake. It certainly is odd to speak of an elemental particle of consciousness, but then elementary particles reveal themselves increasingly to be strange anomolies, quite unlike the tiny BB's we once supposed they were. If science has managed to figure out how to study entities like the massless, uncharged neutrino, we can expect that one day we may develop the capacity to explore the ultimate substance of consciousness.

One of the most important and potentially far-reaching discoveries in particle physics is the puzzling disposition of matter to behave as waves and/or particles. This is another area of research which might possibly be of great significance in the study of death. Wave mechanics has as its primary object one of the most common but least understood phenomena of our experience, namely waves. A wave does not submit easily to philosophical dissection. One's first impression is likely to be that waves are nothing but moving quantities of substance shaped like hills. We can identify a single wave on the ocean and follow it as it travels toward the shore. But a little reflection will show that there is more involved than a traveling hillock of water. When a piece of driftwood is tossed out into the waves it will not move with the wave into shore. It will simply move up and down according to the crest and trough of the wave passing beneath it. The same is true of the water which makes up a wave. We can create waves simply by shaking a rope up and down. The waves travel from our hand out toward the end of the rope. Yet no segment of that rope actually moves out toward the end. Waves, although composed of material substance, or perhaps more accurately, expressed through a physical medium, are not really identical with that substance. A single wave somehow retains its identity while continually changing its material components. The wave, then, is a genuinely puzzling entity. It is to be identified neither with the physical substance which momentarily composes it, nor with the totality of substances through which it eventually expresses itself. A wave is not identical with the entire piece of rope, for example. It is something else. But what? It will not do to say that waves are myths or a species of category mistake. They continue to roll on.

We are not sure exactly how it is that a wave is related to its physical medium, but there is obviously some relationship.

It may occur to the reader at this point that there appears to be an analogy between the problems involved in the understanding of waves and those of another area we have been considering at some length. Perhaps the wave-particle problem is more than coincidentally similar to the mind-body problem. Particles are obviously kin to the body. The body is, in fact, composed of particles. Perhaps waves are kin to the mind. They do seem to bear closer resemblance to properties associated with consciousness than do particles. Perhaps waves:particles=mind:body, or equally, waves:mind=particles:body.[9] Of course this is speculation based upon extraordinarily marginal data, but the prospects are exciting. If we can reach an understanding of exactly how it is that a wave is related to a particle and how they interact with each other we just might be on the way to explaining how the mind and the body interact. Further, and most significant for our purposes here, the question of what happens to the mind when the body dies might begin to be resolved by studying what happens to a wave when its particulate expression is lost. When we drop a pebble in still water we create waves in expanding concentric circles. We can destroy those waves simply by dropping another pebble into them. The particular identifiable waves are destroyed, of course, but they are immediately resolved into other wave patterns which continue their journey. Is it too much to suspect that there are metaphysical implications here?

Another area which deserves more extensive analysis and evaluation comes to us via chemistry. The experiences of chemically induced altered states of consciousness might be of some significance in understanding death. The widespread aversion to the drug culture's affirmation of "better living through chemistry" should not cause us to ignore the possibilities of better metaphysics through chemistry. The various psychedelic substances, such as LSD-25 and mescaline, promise a magical mystery tour into the deepest and most carefully hidden recesses of the mind. The term "psychedelic" means, literally, mind-manifesting. It may legitimately be doubted that there is any significance to the "revelations" claimed on behalf of these drugs, but this doubt should be based upon something more adequate than some *a priori* rejection of a counter-culture. In fact, although there are serious legal restrictions in this area, some interesting research has been done in the exploration of death with psychedelic drugs.

Undoubtedly, the most significant studies have been made by the late Dr. Walter Pahnke, whose work with mind-altering drugs was innovative and pioneering. Pahnke held both a Ph.D. in religion and an M.D., thereby bringing to his research a solid background in theology and science. His research with psychedelics quickly convinced him that their potential value extended far beyond their interesting chemical properties and the unusual reactions they seemed to release. Pahnke believed that they might prove to be a valuable key to some of the deeper mysteries in metaphysics, including such obscure areas as mysticism and death. Pahnke did much of his work at the Maryland Psychiatric Research Center, located in Catonsville, Maryland. Many had noted that subjects who underwent psychedelic experiences often claimed to have "died." They even provided descriptions of their experience of death. With the obvious proviso that these descriptions may well be false, the mere possibility that the essence of death may be experienceable within the range of our earthly life merits further study. Unfortunately (for our interests), Pahnke directed his efforts toward the use of psychedelic drugs as a kind of chemotherapy which might be useful in helping bring a dying person to terms with his impending death. There was no sustained effort to determine whether there were metaphysical implications in the reported experiences. Although not strictly classified as analgesics or pain-killers, psychedelic substances such as LSD-25 seem to have pain-killing (or at least pain-ignoring) properties. They often led the subject to a more creative and personally satisfying understanding of himself and his fate. The apparent insight was usually observed to last far beyond the period of time during which the drug was chemically active. The subjects nearly always were helped toward a psychological state of genuine serenity and acceptance of what otherwise might have been an overwhelming experience. As a pharmacological tool to ease the trauma of dying, psychedelic substances deserve the most intensive consideration and study.

But our interests lie elsewhere. What about the claimed revelations which are born from the psychedelic experience? The possibility that these may be veridical or even merely useful in developing a more adequate understanding of metaphysics should not be ignored. If the psychedelic drugs are really mind-manifesting, as they are etymologically supposed to be, it is conceivable that what they reveal about death may be more than mythologically interesting. As we have insisted, perhaps *ad nauseam*, the mysteries of death are inseparable from the ontological status of the mind. It would seem to follow, therefore, that anything which promises a greater understanding of the mechanics of mind promises to be highly significant in unraveling the metaphysical tangles of death. If there is some, admittedly odd, sense in which death might be experienced by the living with the aid of LSD and its chemical kith and kin, the philosopher should eagerly be looking over the shoulders of those doing research in this area.

With the tragically premature death of Dr. Pahnke in a scuba diving accident in 1971, the major responsibility for further research at the Catonsville center was assumed by Dr. Stanislav

Grof, a Czechoslovakian-born psychiatrist, who was no stranger to the wonders of LSD. As a volunteer subject in an early experiment with the drug at the Psychiatric Research Institute in Prague, Dr. Grof had an ecstatic experience of unity, probably similar to the mystical experience of absolute oneness. The power and significance of that experience has never left him. Dr. Grof believes that the psychedelic experience sometimes includes specific, identifiable orientations toward death. The usual understanding of death as the irrevocable, final terminus of experience is replaced by something quite different. Death is seen as a transition from one mode of existence to another. The experience often includes a combination of elements from mysticism and Jungian psychology—e.g., ecstasy, cosmic unity, and transpersonal episodes closely resembling Jung's concepts of a collective unconscious repository of racial memories and archetypes. Are these insights valid? The question is premature. It can presumably be answered only by independent corroboration or perhaps by undergoing the experience oneself. We are not yet capable of choosing the first option, and it is illegal to exercise the second. Grof's own response to the question is noncommittal: "Whether these are valid insights into the nature of reality, or merely merciful delusions, I don't think we can say for certain."[10] Pahnke himself has written that the psychedelic experience is "characterized by astonishingly lucid thought."[11] While he stops short of committing himself to the factual accuracy of such thought, he does make a startling claim: "This knowledge is not an increase in facts but is a gain in psychological, philosophical, or theological insight."

Dr. Henry K. Beecher, of the Harvard medical school, has quite correctly objected to the boldness of that statement. "What and where is the evidence for this?" he asks.[12] Others have resisted embracing the "insights" of such experiments on the reasonable grounds that we have not developed adequate standards by which they might be judged. But the suggestion that further exploration of the possible significance of psychedelic experiences for our understanding of death is needed does not rest upon the assumption that these revelations are true. Nor should we be required to provide definitive means of judging such experiences before psychedelic research is allowed. It is certainly true that the development of some criteria by which reasonable men could evaluate the metaphysical claims in this area is important and must eventually be made. But at this point it is a matter of data. In order for us to build reasonable hypotheses in metaphysics it is important that we have extensive data at our disposal. Whatever the final truth may be, it must be consistent with all that we know. Whether the claims of Pahnke's subjects are valid or not cannot yet be determined. But that such claims are made is in itself significant. The issue simply cannot be settled without analysis. The data must be gathered and evaluated in terms of their internal consistency and their coherence with other things we know to be true. But the data must be gathered.

The intriguing possibility raised by experiments with psychedelic drugs really centers around the claim that death may be an experienceable event within the earthly life-span of an individual. A similar suggestion was made earlier in this chapter when we examined hypnotism and psychoanalysis as potential sources of knowledge about death. But other suggestions along this line have been made, and they bear serious consideration. The study of psychology has led to an examination of a type of experience which in many ways closely parallels what some of Pahnke's patients reported. It also resembles, and indeed may be identical with, certain types of mystical experiences. It has been referred to variously as cosmic consciousness, peak experience, absorption, and field consciousness. Such experiences are most common during periods of unusual psychological stress or an unusual lack of stress during meditation, although they might occur at any time for no obvious reason. In part, these experiences seem to involve a sense of having undergone death. It would perhaps be more precise to speak of ego-death, in order to avoid the conceptual difficulties of thinking that it is possible to experience death as a total extinction. It is apparently possible to experience ego death as a loss of the sense of self as a specific, identifiable entity, in favor of a "larger" experience-able reality. When this happens, the subject invariably describes the experience in terms relating to death. Certainly if our initial assumptions about the nature of the self entail the belief that the ego represents the total reality of an individual, such experiences must be discounted as deceptions, illusions, or misinterpreta-tions. After all, there must be something left to receive the experience, and what could that be except the ego? The difficulty here is that there is simply too much information which suggests that the ego as we understand it may not be identical with the self in a final, total, and absolute sense. This claim is as ancient as recorded history, but it has been taken seriously by many scholars in our own time. The studies of Sigmund Freud forced him to broaden his own understanding of the self beyond the ego to his well-known theories of the deeper layers of the subconscious. Paul Tillich would feel quite comfortable with the suggestion that such expanded notions of the self are similar to his concepts of ultimate reality in that they point in the direction of that which serves as the ground of our being. The point, of course, is that it would be quite illegitimate to dismiss *a priori* the possibility that death may have to do with one level of the self, while leaving untouched whatever deeper levels there might be. There is no compelling reason to do this apart from the assumption that the self is identical with the ego.

But since that is precisely the issue, an open mind is called for at this point.

If death is an experienceable event within the boundaries of life, the implications are awesome. W. G. Roll, who prefers to speak of such an experience as "field consciousness," scores a bull's-eye when he writes "if it should be found that field consciousness transcends space-time barriers, including the moment of death, survival after death could in effect be reached before."[13] He goes on to suggest that such experiences might prove valuable for the sense of expansion and cosmic understanding that they seem to provide and possibly as a means of training or preparing for our final exit from this world. But the real significance of such a possibility for a philosophy of death is to be found in its potential for research. If an experience of death is attainable in the living, it seems reasonable to suppose that the living might pursue such an experience in order to better understand it. A more thorough examination of this experience will be provided in the following chapter. But it seems safe at this stage to conclude that death may not necessarily remain an ultimately inscrutable mystery.

Most people in our time have assumed that the metaphysics of death is at best a subject of unverifiable speculation, amounting to nothing more than an attempt to translate our unfounded hopes and biases into intellectually respectable wording. No actual definitive solution to the puzzle is even theoretically possible, it is believed. This may be one reason that the question of death, while obviously of paramount importance, has not been thoroughly and systematically considered by the mainstream of philosophy and science. An adequate understanding of death as a metaphysical event has been given the status of a LaManchian impossible dream, to be pursued only by those who are willing to tilt with windmills. The purpose of this chapter has been to suggest that such an attitude, while understandable, may no longer be valid. It is predicated upon the discredited notion that "progress" is the special prerogative of technology, forever denied to metaphysics.

But it is important to note that there have been significant and startling advances in our understanding of the cosmos and these have had serious implications with respect to how we should understand ourselves. The conceptual difficulties involved in coming to terms with the data of physics and astronomy seem to parallel the more traditional philosophical and psychological attempts to understand the mind and its relationship to the body. The earliest speculations of philosophy moved quickly to this very issue. One of the least satisfying elements of Plato's metaphysics is his effort to explain the relationship between the dual aspects of reality as he identified them. The Platonic realm of Forms is clearly mental in nature. In fact, Plato referred to this realm as the world of *ideai,* a Greek word from which our word "idea" is obviously derived. His world of appearances is basically what Descartes meant by extended substance. It was obvious to Plato that a comprehensive account of reality as we experience it must ignore neither the mental nor the physical. The main weakness in Platonic thought is to be found in the attempts to explain just how it is that the world of extended substance can have anything to do with the world of ideas. Plato speaks vaguely of physical objects as "shadows" or "reflections" or "images" somehow "participating" in their essential reality which is to be found in the realm of the Forms. But there is no clear explanation of what these terms mean. In fact, in one of the most remarkable pieces of philosophical literature, the *Parmenides,* Plato presents devastating (and unanswered!) criticisms of his own theory at exactly this point. But his ambiguous accounts of the relationship between the two realms is certainly no worse than that provided by Descartes, who was trying to understand the connection between the mind and the body. The philosophically embarrassing retreat to the pineal gland as the locus of some sort of miraculous interaction between thinking and extended substance is not even as satisfying as Platonic participation. This, of course, is the enigma of the mind-body problem in philosophy which even today seems not to have advanced much beyond the resolution given by Plato.

But the failure of twenty-five hundred years of philosophy to provide a definitive answer to this issue does not mean that we have been marking time in idle speculation. Nor does it at all imply that an answer is unattainable. Further, the suggestion here is that much of the latest work in science is quite relevant to what has traditionally been considered the philosophical problem of the relationship between the mind and the body. Contemporary physics and astronomy are, after all, largely metaphysics. It should be clear that no final account of death is possible until we better understand the mind and its relationship to the body. If the suggestion that such an understanding may be facilitated by further research into the nature of submicroscopic particles is a reasonable one, it would also seem reasonable to call for greater efforts in this direction. "Theoretical" science is not so impractical as some have believed. Such speculations may be critical in helping us move toward a rational philosophy of death. They carry the hope that scientists and philosophers may be converging toward an intellectual omega point in which the ultimate nature of the self can be discovered. It would be quite unreasonable to hope for a "Manhattan Project" exploration of the mind and its status in death. Our culture is nowhere near the point of being ready to devote its major investigative resources to the questions of philosophy. But such pressures are already building and may increase to the point where they cannot be ignored. The possibility of exploring the realms of metaphysics, not only through subjective philosophical speculation but also with objective laboratory research, is just too exciting for us to avoid someday taking it seriously.

It has not been the purpose of this chapter to suggest that these are the only ways in which science and philosophy might cooperate in the study of death. There are other promising areas which might prove to be more fruitful than any mentioned here. Our main purpose has been to combat the notion held by the great majority of people, including most philosophers, that the questions of metaphysics can never be resolved conclusively. Someday we may be released from the ultimately unsatisfying necessity of answering the questions of death with an educated guess, grounded finally in gut-level feelings or hunches. If the human entity is not carrying a fatal flaw and mankind manages to survive its own tendencies, perhaps we will go on to understand death as well as, or better than, the composition of water. There is no compelling reason to assume that genuine metaphysical knowledge is forever denied to the inquiring mind. There has already been motion toward a reunion of philosophy and the fragmented, departmentalized scientific disciplines which exist today. Philosophy has been called the Queen of the sciences. Can she be forever separated from her honored subjects? At one level it appears that the Milesian monists were basically correct. Ultimate reality, or truth, is what it is (whatever it is). It is one. It would therefore seem that those who pursue the truth, down whatever paths they have chosen, must finally meet, for they have the same goal. It is a fascinating prospect, for not only would we be exploring the mysteries of death through a cooperation of philosophy, theology, and science, we would be probing the nature of God.

CHAPTER 7
Ego Death

We are ready now to consider in some depth an area which should serve a dual purpose for us. It will sharpen our perception of just what is involved in the occasion of death by directing our attention to the specific quality of death which seems to generate our greatest fears about it. It will further continue our efforts of the last chapter by focusing our thoughts on an area which might be pursued by philosophers and scientists to mutual advantage. This chapter is concerned with the concept of ego death.

On one level, ego death is precisely what we have been meaning by death itself. It involves a loss of the sense of self, or personal ego—the extinction of that which is not only the most important thing about a person, it *is* the person. One who undergoes ego death is no longer aware of any "I" or "me," nor is he aware of anything else. In this respect, ego death is quite indistinguishable from what is meant by death as we have been considering it. Ego death contains the very roots of our fears about death itself. We have and are, after all, only ourselves, and death presents itself as a threat at just this point. We fear the loss of the only thing we have, namely what we are—i.e., our ego. Ego death carries with it the very heart of our fears about death.

But ego death is more than a loss of the sense of self. It is also a sense of the loss of self. The distinction is far more profound than one of grammatical sequence. In ego death there is an *experience* of the loss of the ego. There is an *experience* of the loss of objects of awareness. The subject *senses* that the I or the me is no more. He has an experience in which subject-object relationships dissolve, and there is, therefore, no awareness of any objects which might allow the subject to identify himself against them. But he is not dead. That is to say, he is not utterly extinguished as might be the case in death. It is difficult to imagine what might be left once the ego has been negated, but the claim is that something is left and no philosophy of death can avoid studying the implications of ego death.

The concept of ego death is basically grounded in mysticism. It is, in fact, the very goal of the mystical experience. Meditation aims at the elimination of all sensory input, all objects of thought. But meditation does not aim at falling asleep. At this point, one of the most important controversies in philosophical thought comes into focus. Philosophy has always had as a basic motivation the search for an understanding of the self. Every philosopher has, at least in passing, given some sort of answer to the question, Who (or what) am I? There are, of course, many possible answers, but I would like to suggest that there are two very basic answers that have been given such that other answers have been rather like variations on one or the other of these themes. In what might be a somewhat arbitrary selection of spokesmen, I will cite two British philosophers of the empiricist tradition as representatives of these two basic positions. In their respective concepts of the self John Locke and David Hume clash head on. Their beliefs in this matter appear so incompatible as to be contradictions of each other. No compromise here seems possible. They present a genuine and profoundly significant issue, and, although we cannot now be certain which position is correct, there is at least the possibility that the issue will one day be resolved conclusively. The issue has to do with the nature of the mind. The catchphrase associated with Locke is the *tabula-rasa,* the belief that the mind is like a blank tablet. Locke formulated his ideas of the mind as a *tabula rasa* primarily in order to deny the prevailing Cartesian notion of innate ideas. Locke meant to deny that there are innate ideas by developing the concept of the mind as analogous to a blank tablet which then receives, via the senses, whatever ideas it might have. But it is really something else that interests us here. Locke is committed to the position that it makes sense to speak of mental substance, or awareness (i.e., the tablet), apart from the ideas or impressions that it may have (i.e., the *blank* tablet). Locke did not really pursue his idea at this point, but it is clear that an understanding of the mind as a blank tablet does allow for the possibility of mental reality—sheer, raw awareness—without objects of awareness, without ideas of any kind.

It was here that David Hume, another British empiricist, spotted a basic weakness in Locke's concept of the *tabula rasa.* Empirical philosophy is grounded solidly in experience as the source of knowledge. It is a tradition which insists that it is meaningless to claim knowledge of something which has not been experienced. We must be able to trace all legitimate concepts to their source in sense experience. Where, asks Hume, is there a sense experience of Locke's *tabula rasa?* Can we find an impression, or an experience, of a self apart from whatever ideas the self may have? In other words, Hume, before he will accept Locke's notion that there is a self which receives impressions (like a tablet which receives markings), demands that such an entity be discovered via experience. Hume makes the attempt, and the result is a disaster for Locke's concept of the *tabula rasa.* "For my part, when I enter most intimately into what I call *myself,* I always stumble on some particular perception or other, of heat or cold, light or shade, love or hatred, pain or pleasure. I can never catch *myself* at any time without a perception, and never can observe anything but the perception."[1] Since Locke places himself in the empirical tradition, Hume's empirical attack upon his concept of the *tabula rasa* is well taken. A little reflection will reveal to the reader that Locke would have a difficult time indeed should he attempt to discover an impression of the self apart from any and all impressions!

The relevance of this issue for our present purposes is simply this. The mystical tradition, with which the concept of ego death is generally associated, must initially ally itself with Locke. If Hume is correct, then the entire thrust of mysticism would appear to be in a thoroughly hopeless direction. Let us examine more closely the concept of ego death in the mystical tradition in order to clarify this point.

The various meditative disciplines—Yoga, for example— attempt gradually to eliminate all sense data and all objects of thought. This is done in a very systematic way. The subject first selects an object of thought upon which he will make an effort to concentrate all of his attention, the whole of his mental energies. This sounds like precisely the opposite of what he ultimately desires—i.e., the elimination of all such objects of thought— and in fact it is. But this is only a first step toward the final end. A subject may choose to concentrate on his own breathing, for example, or a meaningless concept like the sound of one hand clapping or the shape of his face before he was born. He may concentrate on the flame of a candle or a paradoxical riddle. Or he may select a mantra, a sequence of sounds, which he will repeat to himself over and over and over. There are many options. The point is that if one can focus one's attention exclusively upon a single idea, he will be able to ignore and thereby eliminate other impressions which would ordinarily compete for attention. This much really does make a certain kind of sense. We have all had the experience of concentrating our attention upon a given subject to the extent that we literally became unaware of whatever was going on around us. Usually the subject must be inherently fascinating or at least of overwhelming importance (studying for a final exam, for example) in order for us to be able to give our attention exclusively to it. In meditation the object of concentration should not be fascinating or important for reasons which will become apparent. This shows why discipline is so necessary in meditation. It is not easy to devote our minds entirely to something as trivial as counting our breaths, but that is just what is required. As the subject becomes successful in focusing his awareness upon a single point he will find that other extraneous thoughts which ordinarily would ebb and flow through his consciousness are ignored. It is, to use Locke's analogy, a process in which the myriad impressions on the tablet are gradually erased until, if the meditation is successful, only a single impression remains. Let us suppose that the disciple of meditation has succeeded in reducing his impressions to a single point—his mantra or whatever he has chosen as a means to the final goal. The tablet, of course, is not yet blank. There remains the single point. There is still a subject-object distinction, an awareness and the object of that awareness. So far, few people would have any quarrel with the claims of meditation to this point. It certainly is possible to reach a mental state in which the field of awareness has only a single object. It may be difficult to devote our attention to a trivial object, but it does not seem to be impossible. Further, if it can be done, it seems reasonable to accept the claim that all other objects of awareness have indeed been eliminated.

The next step is not so easily accepted. The goal of meditation is ego death. This involves a total erasure of the tablet. So long as there is a single impression remaining, the process of meditation has not yet been completely successful. As Descartes has shown, if there is an object of thought, there is the thinker. And if there is the thinker, there is the ego. What, then, is the next step? The claim is that continued concentration upon the single point will eventually result in the elimination of that point. This might be clarified if we think about the many times we have looked into the skies on a dark and cloudless night. If we pick out a single star and stare at it, we will find that it has a tendency to disappear. In order to pick it up again we will have to look away from it slightly. Some very faint stars simply cannot be seen by looking at them directly. When we do, they fade from our vision. The idea in meditation is, perhaps, similar in this respect. As we concentrate intensely upon the single point, the star-point of our awareness, it too will disappear. And the tablet will be blank.

What will be left? Here the issue between Locke and Hume is joined. According to Hume, there could be nothing left once all impressions have been erased. The subject will fall over in a stupor of unconsciousness or else he will be dead. In no way can Hume allow for the possibility that there might be consciousness without any objects of thought. Hume must insist that, if there is awareness, there is necessarily awareness *of*. The concept of pure consciousness without an object simply has no place in Humean metaphysics. If Hume is correct, then not only is Locke wrong, the entire aim of mysticism is refuted. For the mystics insist that the state of awareness without an object of awareness can be achieved and that it is not a state of unconsciousness. It is, in fact, a variation of Locke's *tabula rasa*. It is not identical with Locke's concept because Locke believed that this was the real self in an ego sense. The *tabula rasa* is Locke's way of understanding the individual, identifiable self—the ego. The mystics, while rejecting Hume's belief that there is nothing other than impressions, would also disagree with Locke at this point. The ego, much as Hume predicted, would be gone with the disappearance of the final impression. There is no ego apart from the ideas. The individual self is really the specific set of ideas and impressions, as Hume said. But Hume clearly rejects the idea that there might be a mental substratum underlying those ideas. Bertrand Russell suggested an analogy which might help here. He said that Locke understood the mind as analogous to a string onto which various beads of experience (ideas) were strung. The string, then, is Locke's "self." Hume, being unable to locate an impression of the string, simply pulls it out. The self, on Hume's analysis, consists only of the beads. Elimination of the beads (as in meditation) eliminates all that there is to us if Hume is correct. If Locke is correct, elimination of the beads would reveal the raw, pure, unadulterated mind, the self. Mysticism must basically cast its lot with Locke. The mystic denies that we are finally our ideas, our impressions. There is a *tabula rasa,* although this is not to be understood as being possessed exclusively by the self, the individual ego. The *tabula rasa* is not the self as ego, but rather the Self as cosmic consciousness. It is what Aldous Huxley called Mind-at-Large. It is what the Hindu calls Brahman. It is what Jung terms the collective unconscious. It is not the specific, identifiable ego. It is, in fact, the Ultimate Reality behind each individual ego.

Let us suppose, for the moment, that this all makes some kind of sense. Let us assume that it is possible to attain a cosmic awareness in which the experience of the self is lost in favor of a larger, perhaps somehow a universal, consciousness. What would this entail? Let us look at it this way. What is the self (small *s*), after all? Perhaps we can begin to understand the ego if we consider what it is that separates it from the rest of reality. We do seem to put a handle on the ego by dividing the universe into the me and the not-me. It may be that those qualities which make such a division possible form the basis for our concept of the ego. What is it that distinguishes me from the not-me? What are these differentiating qualities which allow me to identify myself within the whole of reality? It is not overly difficult to identify them. The problem is not that they are obscure and hidden, but rather that they are too obvious. For example, I am clearly separated from all other things by the physical substance of which I (and not anything else) am composed. I am made out of this hunk of meat, and you are not. Nothing else in the universe is made from the same material as that which forms my body. One might object that certain individual cells in my body are made from the same material. But I, as an organic whole, am identical only with that whole, and it really makes no difference that my body contains within it certain subsets of entities. No proper subset is identical with the whole, and it is the whole that we are concerned with.

Certainly we must acknowledge a debt to Hume by noting that my experiences and ideas are shared by no one and nothing else. The totality of my ideas, then, must count as another of my differentiating qualities. They help me to spot "me" as opposed to anything else.

There are at least two other rather obvious properties which set me apart from all else, namely my spatial and temporal locations. I am located in space and time in such a way as to set me apart from other things. I am here, and you are there. We cannot both occupy the same place at the same time. But it might be pointed out that I do share a temporal location with other things and this would then not properly be identified as a differentiating quality. I exist at a specific moment in time and so does every other currently existing thing. Time is admittedly a strange differentiating quality. I do share with my typewriter and this chair existence at the present moment. Yet I am also separated in time from certain other things that are not me. I do not, for example, occupy the same temporal location as George Washington. He lived then, and I live now. I do not share the same point of time as the seventy-fifth president of the United States. He or she, presumably, has not yet been born, and when that blessed event takes place I expect to be long gone. The list of differentiating qualities could easily be extended indefinitely if we were content to identify literally all the things which distinguish me from everything else. But the basic qualities which form the boundaries by which I am identified are the four mentioned above: (1) matter, (2) totality of ideas, (3) location in space, and (4) location in time.

Remember, now, that the goal of meditation is specifically the elimination of one of these differentiating qualities—i.e., the totality of my ideas. Assume for the moment that such a thing is possible, and that the mystic can achieve a state accurately described as awareness without an object. He would then have succeeded in erasing all impressions from the tablet, or, to follow Russell's analogy, removed all the beads from the string. If Hume is right, then nothing can be left. There is no tablet, there is no string. There simply can be no awareness without being aware of something. But if Hume is wrong, and he might be, then the species of awareness that might be left would be a very strange breed indeed. The mystic claims that, at this point, there would be the achievement of ego death. Let us examine that claim. Assuming that there is a basic substratum of awareness left after the elimination of all ideas, what would the nature of that form of consciousness be? It has been called by many names—cosmic consciousness, the pure Self, etc. Once the totality of ideas is erased, the only qualities which might separate me from the rest of reality would be matter and location in space/time. If it is possible to experience pure consciousness, that is, if it is possible to be (intensely) aware, without being aware *of* anything, what then becomes of matter? Certainly it does not disappear, but it is clearly eliminated from one's mental fabric. One who experiences pure consciousness cannot in any way sense his material structure, nor can he have an impression of the physical substance of any other thing since all such ideas have supposedly been eliminated. He should be absolutely unable to use matter as a means by which to identify himself in opposition to anything else. He would not, then, be aware of a separation from other objects in this respect. Physical substance would no longer serve as a differentiating quality.

If that is the case, then what possible sense could be made of spatial location as an identifying property? It would seem that only material things could have spatial location. It is simply incredible to suppose that we might somehow triangulate on a nonphysical entity. It is quite inconceivable how one might go about providing coordinates for a nonmaterial essence, which is just what pure consciousness would have to be. The subject who has attained to such a state cannot sense himself as distinct from anything else on the basis of his material substance, since he has negated this possibility through the elimination of objects of thought, including any idea of material substance. Whatever is left could not have any spatial location because such a concept depends upon there being material entities which might have a location in space. The only possible differentiating quality left at this point would be a temporal distinction.

Time is a difficult concept to analyze. It is generally experienced as having a triune quality. We remember the past. We experience the present. We anticipate the future. The sense of time depends upon the distinction of the present moment from the past and the future. If we were to lose continually all memories of past events and if we were absolutely unable to anticipate the future we could experience only the now. Looked at in another way, that is all we can ever hope to experience anyway. We never experience the past except as a present memory. We cannot experience the future except as a present anticipation. When all the dust has settled, all we ever have is the now. The past exists only as a present memory, the future only as a present sense of anticipation. But memory and the sense of anticipation are ideas, and ego death involves a negation of all ideas, including these. In what mode can time be experienced, then, for one who is in a state of pure awareness? There can only be what Tillich has called the "eternal now." In this sense time can indeed be transcended. All time would be as the present to one experiencing ego death. But then time could not possibly serve as a differentiating quality.

Notice, now, that something quite startling has happened. We are, of course, assuming that it is possible to attain to a state of awareness without an object. That is debatable, but if it is true, then such a state would necessarily imply the elimination of precisely those qualities which we have identified as separating us from the rest of reality. Ego death entails the negation of these differentiating qualities. These are the qualities which define the ego. They serve as the parameters of one's self, perhaps also serving as an obstacle to an experience of the Self. It is no wonder that the mystic prattles on about becoming one with the One. There would be no other choice if awareness without an object is possible. If consciousness is somehow still in force during ego death, it would necessarily involve a sense of union. The boundaries of the ego and of all other things are dissolved—in favor of what? Well, it depends upon whether Hume or Locke is correct. Hume would predict that any successful elimination of ideas or impressions (that is, objects of awareness) must result in a state of nonconscious being. He would not necessarily deny that such a process is possible, but he has clearly committed himself to the position that the state of awareness always implies an awareness *of*. For this reason Hume rejected the concept of the *tabula rasa;* it made no empirical sense to him. The *tabula rasa,* on Hume's analysis, was nothing more than an ungrounded, and therefore unwarranted, assumption that there must be something which ties our ideas together, something which serves as an unchanging substratum for the continually changing flow of our experience. We suppose that this flow of experience is happening to *us*. I tend to think, after all, that it is *I* who am receiving the experiences which come to me and that it is this *I* (the tablet, or the string, or the ego) which abides throughout the flux of experience. But since we can never "catch" this self apart from the impressions produced by experience, Hume naturally draws the conclusion demanded by empirical philosophy that the concept is mistaken. He believes we are identifying ourselves with a purely fictitious entity. There is a self, to be sure. But Hume believes that we need go no further than our experiences to find it. We are our impressions. We are our experiences. It is the set of ideas themselves which defines the individual, and it is unnecessary to conjure up a mysterious mental substratum, of which we can never have an experience or an impression, in order to locate the ego. The loss of those impressions is the loss of the self. Locke, of course, could insist that the loss of such impressions would leave us with the *tabula rasa,* the mental tablet erased clean of all impressions.

It should be clear now that those who have worked with the concept of ego death would not agree entirely with Hume. They deny that awareness is necessarily dual in nature, that is, that there must be a subject-object quality to all awareness as Hume insists. They maintain that something is left subsequent to the elimination of all impressions, although, interestingly, they often refer to it by using the term "the void." The void, however, is not understood as the absolute negation of reality itself, but rather the final vision of reality beyond the lesser, transient plurality of ordinary experience. But there is a point at which the mystic who advances the cause of ego death would agree with Hume and thereby disagree with Locke. Hume understood the individual ego as being a particular set of impressions, and the mystic would basically agree. Hume would probably have denied that there can be an experience apart from the individual ego, and the mystic would certainly disagree. The agreement would come at the point at which the definition or understanding of the ego is made. We, as individual selves, are defined by our particular set of impressions. But there is a basic substance underlying all selves which can be experienced apart from all impressions, and therefore only through the death or negation of the ego. This sounds like Locke's *tabula rasa,* and in one sense it is. The experience of ego death is one which has broken through the limits of the ego by eliminating the impressions on the tablet. The cosmic consciousness is a blank slate, absolutely devoid of specific impressions. But Locke is wrong, on the mystic's analysis, when he identifies the blank tablet as the ultimate *individual* substance. There is, and there can be, no individual anything without some differentiating qualities. Since the blank tablet has no such qualities, we must be making a mistake when we identify it with the individual self, as Locke surely meant to do.

All of this should begin to help us understand something about the concept of ego death and perhaps how it relates to some of the other claims made by mystics and others, like reality being one, and the possibility of losing oneself in favor of union with that One. If there is an experience of ego death, it must be an experience of absolute unity. Ego death, by its very nature, negates all which allows a distinction between the me and the not-me. Ego death and the world of plurality and multiplicity are simply incompatible. If ego death is achieved, then the manifold quality of the world must go. But the reverse is also true. So long as we have an experience of diversity we cannot experience ego death. On this analysis, there is a legitimate distinction between one's self and the Self. One's self is properly differentiated from all other selves. One's self more than belongs to one—it *is* one. The Self can belong to no one, since it is no individual entity set apart from another. This is why we never come across references to "my Self," or "your Self," and so on. The mystic speaks of *"the* Self." Huxley never writes about "my mind-at-large," but rather "Mind-at-Large," without even an individuating "the," since Mind-at-Large is the property of no single individual and is not itself a thing among other things. It is obvious that we do not and cannot experience the Self in a perception. We cannot experience the Self via Humean impressions, and this is precisely why Hume was unable to "catch *myself* at any time without a perception." There are two reasons for this. First, the individual ego is, as Hume says, the perceptions which serve to distinguish it from other things. The concept, therefore, of "myself . . . without a perception" is something like the concept of a triangle without three sides. Since the individual ego is identical with the perceptions which set it apart, there is no way Hume should have been able to spot the ego without a perception. Second, the Self cannot be found through such a procedure either, since the Self cannot be experienced until all perceptions have been eliminated. But Hume was not trying to eliminate all perceptions. He was trying to *examine* his perceptions, or perhaps peek between them, in order to discover if there might be some sort of Lockean *tabula rasa*. He was, on his own terms, looking for a perception of the ego-without-a-perception.

Hume, then, could not possibly have succeeded in detecting either himself—i.e., his own individual ego—or the Self, apart from his perceptions. This is not because there is no individual ego, nor is it because there is no Self. It is rather the very nature of these two terms which dictated the outcome of his efforts. While we experience plurality, while we are aware of the multiplicity of ideas in our minds, we are directly experiencing the ego, since that is precisely what the ego is. But while we are experiencing, or examining, these perceptions, it is simply not possible to have an experience of the Self. In fact the *very process* of trying to observe the Self is, if the reader will excuse me, self-defeating. In other words, Hume was trying to do what cannot possibly be done.

Now this is a very strong claim. I have argued that it is not just difficult, but logically impossible, for Hume or anyone else to observe, detect, or discover the Self. The reason is simply that such a procedure necessarily involves a duality. There must be the observer (Hume) and the thing observed (the Self). But an experience of the Self is not possible so long as there are any distinctions at all, including that of observer and observee. Wherever there is plurality of any kind, whether spatial (here and there), temporal (past, present, and future), material (this and that), or epistemological (subject and object), there is no Self. This is not because the Self is obstinate and refuses to show up during any experience of plurality, but rather because it *cannot* show up under such circumstances, since it is incompatible with them. Furthermore, since duality is a kind of plurality, even the distinction between one's self and the Self cannot be present during the experience of ego death. Having an idea of the Self is not the equivalent of knowing the Self. Hume had an idea of the Self, at least in a Lockean sense, since he was able to determine that he could not "catch" it. He knew enough about what he was after to know that he did not find it. He thereupon concluded that such a concept had no referent—it did not exist. For Hume, as for most of us, knowledge involves an observer understanding a thing observed, or a knower grasping that which is known. If the Self cannot be observed, how can it be known? Hume concluded that it could not be known, and therefore to speak of it made no sense.

But there is, and indeed there must be, a type of knowledge which does not require such dualistic observation. Descartes distinguished between two types of knowledge. He identified deductive knowledge as that which is derived from something else which is known. It is the conclusion yielded by certain premises. It obviously involves at least the plurality of premise and conclusion, and therefore the Self, if it can be known at all, cannot be known via the deductive process. But if all knowledge is deductive, then it can be shown that there is no knowledge at all. The conclusion gained from the premises of an argument can be no more certain than those premises. The premises will themselves have to be deduced from other premises, which will, in turn, have to be based upon certain other premises, and so it goes. If all knowledge is deductive then we can simply never get started, since we generate an infinite regress. One might be tempted to suggest that this does indeed show that there is and can be no knowledge at all, and therefore a complete skepticism is in order. But if we have demonstrated that there is no knowledge at all, it would seem that we are now the proud possessors of at least one bit of knowledge—namely that there is no knowledge. And that has to sound strange. We are forced to admit that Descartes was correct in claiming that there must be another kind of knowledge. We may disagree that it is intuitive knowledge, as he insisted, but we do have to begin somewhere.

The claim that we might know something intuitively rightly generates a certain suspicion on the part of many philosophers. People have claimed intuitive knowledge of a wide range of propositions. Intuition is the philosophical equivalent of the theologian's faith. It can be a refuge for those who cannot otherwise support their beliefs. But the fact is that there must be some intuitive knowledge. There must be some starting point upon which we may legitimately ground subsequent knowledge. Even the logician begins with his axioms. Where is the deductive proof of the Law of Non-contradiction? There must be a source of knowledge which does not depend upon prior knowledge. This would have to be a direct and immediate awareness of a truth which is genuinely "self-evident." Descartes' prime example of such knowledge was his own ego. The unsurpassably strong argument for his own existence was grounded in intuition. He did not deductively draw from the premise "I think" the conclusion "therefore, I am." His knowledge that he existed did not depend upon something else that he knew to be the case. We all experience ourselves in a way we cannot experience anything else. We do not "catch" in an impression the idea of ourselves, and thereby conclude that we do indeed exist. The direct and immediate experience of the thought process itself is enough for us to know that we exist, at least as a sequence of thought and experiences.

If the Self cannot be known deductively for the reasons we have given, must we conclude that it is therefore impossible to know it at all? Certainly not. Since there is another avenue of knowledge available to us, it is just possible that the Self might be known intuitively. That is, we might be able to gain knowledge of the Self directly through the subjective experience of ego death. And of course that is exactly what is claimed by those who have had the experience. If ego death is what it appears to be, then Hume's belief that we can know nothing beyond our own impressions is basically wrong. Even if the individual ego is identical with its specific set of impressions, and even if that ego can therefore never be found apart from its impressions, as Hume claimed, the metaphysics of ego death indicate that the individual ego is grounded in something far more basic, far more significant than the flow of ideas. The mystic claims that the destruction of the individual ego yields an experience of the Self. He further insists that the Self is the ultimate reality, not only of the ego, but of each and every individual thing which is manifest in the plurality of our experience. Ego death is said to provide literally cosmic insight into the nature of reality, and, more important, into our own metaphysical status.   *127*

It is simply impossible at this point to make a definitive judgment on the validity of such claims. By insisting that the Self can be neither perceived nor detected in any way via sense impressions, we very nearly qualify the concept out of existence. Whether there can be a direct experience of the Self beyond the normal subject-object dimension probably cannot be determined unless and until one has the experience for himself. Even then, it is the *interpretation* of that experience which will be, for others and perhaps for the individual himself, the final measure of the validity of that experience. What are the standards for making such an interpretation and a subsequent judgment of the experience? Presumably they are not the standards we use in making our ordinary ego judgments. It sounds a bit too glib to say that the experience is self-justifying, although perhaps that is the case. The question of whether the experience of ego death is possible and the judgment of whether or not it is veridical if it is possible must remain open.

We have been associating the concept of ego death with the mystic tradition, and it would seem that we are justified in doing so. The writings of the mystics indicate fairly specifically that the aim of the discipline is in fact the elimination of the ego in order to experience the cosmic One. We are told that our sense of self and our perception of multiplicity in the world is basically illusory, that there is an ultimate reality of which all else can only be a lesser aspect. But ego death is not the exclusive concern of the mystic. The experience has occurred to people who have not prepared themselves through meditation or any of the disciplinary exercises within mysticism. Sometimes the experience comes to one who is about to die, or who has had an extremely close brush with death. The reports of such people who survive seem to parallel closely the writings of the mystics.

But the concept of ego death is perhaps best known from the study of psychedelic experiences. One of the major criticisms of the psychedelic drugs is that they might destroy the ego. It is true that ego death may be a part of the drug experience. It is also a fact that the apprehension of approaching ego death may send the LSD voyager into an uncontrollable panic resolving itself into hysteria. This is an important argument for the necessity of an experienced guide during the drug trip who can support the endurance of ego death. But the experience itself is really the psychological foundation of a very ancient theme which threads its way into the fabric of virtually all religions—i.e., death and rebirth. The experience of ego death lies at the heart of the paradoxical claim that only one who has died can fully live. "Unless one is born anew, he cannot see the kingdom of God" (John 3:3). Nicodemus was understandably confused by that statement, and when we are honest with ourselves, so are we. Perhaps it is a disservice to Jesus to suppose that he was talking about ego death. But just perhaps it is a far greater disservice to him if we think that he was talking about anything *less* than ego death. The claim is that for one who has undergone ego death this statement loses its paradoxical quality. The mystery is stripped from the concept, and it is supposedly revealed as a profound truth. The surrender of the ego must come as an awesomely shattering and frightening experience. It seems to entail the loss of the one thing most certain and most important, the one thing we can invariably count on—the Cartesian ego.

If that were the end of the matter, it would seem that ego death is ardently to be avoided. But those who have worked with ego death sense that there is more to it than the negative experience of intense fear or confusion. Dr. Stanislav Grof, working with subjects undergoing psychedelic experiences, has concluded from his research that the mystical vision attained through the experience of ego death can produce startling progress toward mental health. The positive benefits of ego death are such that Grof believes that the full advantages of his treatment cannot be achieved without the experience. Much of his research has been with hospitalized psychotics who were given LSD. With these subjects, the experience of ego death is the very goal of his therapeutic efforts. In any case, there is strong evidence that an understanding of the concept of ego death is crucial to an understanding of one's self.

That is just why ego death must be considered whenever we attempt to work toward a philosophy of death. Most of us suspect, even if we claim to believe otherwise, that the loss of our ego is absolutely the worst possible thing that could happen to us, and furthermore that death is precisely that. This accounts for the rather simplistic formulation of the basic question of death: do we survive it? We assume that this is an either/or situation and that our individual egos will either continue beyond the grave or they will not. Furthermore, we assume that if our egos do not survive death, that is the equivalent of absolute and utter extinction. There appears to be no possibility of compromise between these two positions. Many people therefore have a tendency to cling to the idea that they, as individual selves, will continue after death, while at the same time feeling somewhat uncomfortable about the lack of evidence for that belief. There is also a very real question about the desirability of such a situation as that. We might not feel entirely comfortable with the notion that we are, as it were, stuck with ourselves for an endless eternity. We may find, then, that we are desperately embracing an idea, even though it does not quite satisfy our deepest psychological hungers, simply because the only alternative is even worse. The concept of ego death carries with it the hint that the truth of the matter might lie elsewhere. The alternatives of absolute annihilation on the one hand and an endless continuation of our petty and cosmically insignificant selves on the other just may not exhaust the possibilities. Recalling the suggestion made in chapter 6 that our destiny is almost certainly one in which we will be resolved (or perhaps dissolved) into the matrix of Ultimate Reality, whatever that substance may be, we now apprehend as a viable option that Ultimate Reality is in fact something like Tillich's undifferentiated Being-Itself, and that Ultimate Reality is more than coincidentally similar to the mystic's vision of the One. Furthermore, if all of that is the case, then ego death may provide a legitimate window through which we might be able to glimpse a preview of such things as are to come.

CHAPTER 8
Immortality

We seem to be in the position of one who has been given a ticket to a form of entertainment which requires audience participation. We have not been given the script, or, what amounts to the same thing, we have been deluged with competing scripts. We are completely ignorant of the plot. The final outcome is better hidden from us than the most elegant mystery drama. Our involvement in the production has become so intimate and so consuming that rarely do we pause to wonder just how or why we were given the ticket in the first place. Instead, we direct our full attention to the performance required of us, stumbling our way from scene to scene, hoping vaguely that whatever reviews there may be will be favorable, or at least mixed. In those rare moments when we pause to reflect upon our situation we find it to be curious indeed. The inevitable frustration of our efforts often leads us to turn our attention elsewhere with a shrug of resignation and a feeling of "well, that's life."

And it really is not easy. We sense that there is an ending of some sort and that our present performance should reflect that ending, lead into it somehow. What we are doing now should have some connection with the final denouement, lest we find ourselves inappropriately fiddling while Rome burns, or otherwise being just plain ridiculous. We cannot conceivably do justice to the present scene as long as we are ignorant of just how and when and why the final curtain will fall. Yet that seems precisely to be our position. The final scene is not even a blur to us. It is a void. We have entertained any number of beliefs in this matter. It is a cosmic naïveté in our culture which allows to be taken seriously imagery kith and kin to a little log cabin in glory-land, the Celestial City approached by streets paved with gold, illuminated with mega-caret diamonds dazzling the eyes. Perhaps it is a measure of a cultural reluctance to understand reality as a coherent, consistent whole that accounts for an ability in some people to combine a view of ultimate reality as a celestial playpen, complete with fluffy clouds and harps, with vivid imageries of lakes of eternal fire, worms that never die, and perverted sadists in red underwear going about poking the damned with pitchforks. As a final testimony to man's ability to entertain conflicting beliefs, it has even been supposed that this entire scene was somehow choreographed by the creator of the universe—a creator, called wise, merciful, and father, of a universe containing quarks, consciousness, and quasars. And although we may protest that we never seriously embraced such a world view, it is probably the case that there was a time when it, or some equally simplistic variation, constituted our best guess as to the nature of the final scene.

"When I was a child," says Paul, "I spoke like a child, I thought like a child, I reasoned like a child; when I became a man, I gave up childish ways" (I Cor. 13:11). And so, in large measure, have we. For the most part, we are no longer moved by such visions of our final destiny. Even if they have not specifically been rejected, it is enough to point out that we do not adjust our present life-style in any significant way because of them. Our contemporary performance seems not at all modified by our fears of eternal torment or our hopes for everlasting reward. At most, these views remain as atrophied metaphysical appendages on a somewhat more sophisticated cosmology. If they have not yet been excised surgically, they are at least unused, largely unnoticed, and therefore insignificant. Paul compared his childish reasoning to seeing through a glass darkly. He went on to claim that giving up childish ways brought him face to face with the truth. Most of us have not been so fortunate. We, like him, have also given up our childish ways. But the darkness is still there. Death appears to us as an opaque mystery which prevents us from understanding the final direction of our present situation. We are convinced that the resolution will not be found in childish reasoning, but where does that leave us? We seem to be left without a script, to ad lib as best we can in a performance we continue to think is somehow important. We do feel like poor players, strutting our sound and fury on a stage, in a drama which seems to be building toward a climactic whimper of no significance at all.

We may, if we have the stomach for it, pause to consider certain qualities of this drama which present themselves to us as the most basic, the most general, and the most important aspects of reality. The triumph of good over evil, the knowledge of what it means to love and be loved, the pursuit of truth, the attainment of wisdom—these are not treasures which thieves might steal. They are immune to corruption by rust and moth. Yet we can ask of them precisely the question Jesus directed to the man whose sights were set on earthly treasures: Whose will they be? If this night, or any night in the next three-score and ten years, my soul is required of me, whose *will* they be? It is really small comfort to me should I learn that some favored few throughout the entire range of human thought have achieved enlightenment. I am neither a Buddha nor a messiah. Yet I have the same hunger, for I am surely made of the same substance as they. Am I being taunted? Have I been given desires for which there is no satisfaction? Have I been created to be frustrated? Am I condemned to absurdity? It is no answer to point out that I might redouble my efforts, that the fault is within myself, that I lack the single-minded discipline necessary for enlightenment. All of this is near enough to the truth so that I do not deny it. But if, from the countless billions of souls that have been, are, and will be, some few dozens or even thousands have succeeded in attaining to the heights of cosmic insight, what, as a practical matter, is the point in my struggles? I face odds of billions to one. I would not bet an inflated penny on a positive outcome and neither would any sane person. The mocking laughter of death presents a cosmic obstacle to my deepest hopes. I do not hope for a reservation on cloud nine in the seventh heaven. I do not even know what that means. I do not fear the torments of hell, nor do I feel particularly brave in saying so. I do know that I, as a philosopher, but even more as a human being, want to learn what it all means. I am not so concerned that it mean this or that, but whatever it means I want to know. I want to know whether or not there is an ultimate purpose to reality, whether the world has a meaning or whether the existentialists are right in claiming that it is ultimately absurd. I want to know what is behind the distinctions between good and evil. Have we made these concepts up, spinning them from ephemeral webbing produced from the bowels of our own imaginations, or is there an absolute moral difference between Christ and Hitler? I want to know who I am and why I am. I want to know my destiny. In short, I want the whole ball of wax.

We have come to a point in this book where we must finally consider the prospects for immortality. It is, after all, the real issue. The substance of our concern with death is formed around the core of our ignorance as to our status beyond the grave. Whatever final hopes and fears we may have, they simply cannot be unaffected by this issue. Even if we expect to be able to stave off death for many years to come, it is always present with us, not only as a possibility at any moment, but as an inevitability. Our beliefs about death have to affect our present attitudes toward life. What are we? Immortal or ephemeral? Is our soul formed of eternal substance that will outlast even the stars? Or are we blips on a metaphysical screen, grabbing desperately for a pitiful three-score and ten years, which is quickly swallowed up in the maw of infinite time? This is a high-stakes issue. It centers on the question of whether we possess eternal life, and its resolution commands our interest if not our devotion.

But the pursuit of death should not be a rush to metaphysical judgment. The issue is far too complex to allow a successful frontal assault. We are simply going to have to pick it apart, bone by bone, before we can hope to make a reasonable guess as to its structure. In other words, our first task would seem to be an analysis of the concept of immortality.

Etymologically, the word immortality is designed to indicate a negation of, or an exemption from, death—i.e., eternal life. Our initial dissection, then, reveals two basic components of immortality which themselves will require analysis, namely, eternality and life. If we can understand just what is meant by the concept of eternality and how it might apply to a living substance, we should then have a solid idea of what we are talking about as we explore the possibilities for immortality.

Let us consider first the concept of eternality. It seems that we pretty well understand what is meant by the predicate "eternal." If x is eternal, then x is, was, and will always be. But there is much more to it than this. The concept of eternality is closely related to the concept of infinity. It is a relationship of infinity to time. This was recognized from the earliest beginnings of philosophy, but there was often a lot of confusion at this point. Melissus, for example, after arguing eloquently for the notion that reality must be eternal, concludes directly that, since "it is always, so also must its size always be infinite." [1] Few of us would be inclined to make such a logical leap. It certainly does not follow that, because x is temporally infinite, it is therefore spatially infinite. Some of the source of this confusion may be revealed in Melissus' own words: "But since it has neither begun nor ended, it always was and always will be and has no beginning nor end." To say that something "has no beginning nor end" might lead us to conclude that "its size must always be infinite." But it is at least conceivable that an entity, say an eternal star, might exist forever, yet be of finite size. Further, without too great a strain on the imagination, it is conceivable that a reality infinite in size might come into and pass out of existence. The diversity of qualities of infinity must be recognized if we are to avoid confusion. There is surely a difference between temporal infinity and spatial infinity, and the possession of one does not logically guarantee the possession of the other. Certainly, when we are considering the immortality of the soul, we are concerned with infinity as it relates to the temporal mode and not with the spatial dimensions of the soul. The soul may be infinitely extended, or it may have no extension at all. But our concern is with eternality—the infinity of time.

Having focused our attention on the specific concept of infinite time, we will quickly discover that such a concept is not so specific after all. In fact, temporal infinity might be understood in several different ways. The assumption is usually made that an eternal object, in the words of Melissus, "is and always was and always will be." But let us take a closer look. Infinity is really a mathematical concept, and perhaps we should turn our attention to a mathematical analysis in order to understand more clearly the possibilities of infinity.

We can speak of an infinite sequence of numbers, for example, and it would seem that we can pretty well understand what that means. But this is only a "ball-park" understanding. There are many different ways in which a sequence of numbers might be infinite. The sequence might, for example, be unbounded. Taking 0 as a vague sort of middle, we can construct a set of integers which proceeds to infinity on both sides, thus $\{\ldots, -3, -2, -1, 0, +1, +2, +3, \ldots\}$. This sequence has no beginning, since the negative numbers can continue indefinitely. Neither does it have an end, since obviously the positive numbers have no upper limit. But we can construct a set of integers such that the sequence will have a beginning, but no end. It, too, will have an infinite number of members: $\{1, 2, 3, \ldots\}$. This, of course, is the set of natural numbers. It is the sequence of all the positive whole integers. It begins with 1 and proceeds to infinity. If we keep our directions straight, we can construct a set of integers such that the sequence will have an end, but no beginning: $\{\ldots, -3, -2, -1, 0\}$. This is the set of negative numbers. Without waxing too clever we can even construct a set of integers such that the sequence will have a beginning *and* an end, yet the set will still contain an infinite number of members: $\{0, \frac{1}{2}, \frac{3}{4}, \frac{7}{8}, \ldots, 1\}$. This is simply the sequence of fractions between 0 and 1. It begins with 0 and ends with 1, but clearly generates an infinite sequence in between.

Each of these sets has infinitely many members. They all generate an infinite sequence of integers, yet they exhibit significant differences in the type of infinity they represent. For convenience and, we hope, for the sake of clarity, let us refer to the first set, whose members are the negative and positive integers, as Φ (phi). The sequence exhibited by Φ has no beginning and no end. The set containing the sequence of natural numbers has a beginning but no end, and we will call it A (alpha). The set of negative numbers, having an end but no beginning, will be dubbed Ω (omega). The set whose members are the sequence of fractions between 0 and 1, since it has both a beginning and an end, is hereby christened A/Ω (alpha/omega). Now that we have named our sets, they, like children, should be easier to handle.

Further, let us say that when a given concept of infinity exhibits qualities analogous to Φ, it has Φ-infinity. For example, if we imagine a piece of string infinitely long, with no beginning and no end, we will say that it has Φ-infinity. But we can also imagine a piece of string infinitely long which has a beginning, but stretches out an infinite distance and therefore has no end. This piece of string will be said to have A-infinity, for obvious reasons (it is vaguely similar to the set A). We can further imagine a piece of string having an end but no beginning, since it stretches infinitely toward its source. This piece of string exhibits Ω-infinity, although it is a bit difficult to see how it really differs from the piece of string having A-infinity. But that is not our problem. Finally, it is possible to imagine a piece of string infinitely long, having both a beginning and an end. Suppose you are holding a piece of string, one end in each hand, and someone takes hold of the middle and begins to pull it out away from you. Suppose further (this is not cheating, since we really can imagine it) that the string is made of a substance which allows it to stretch indefinitely. It is conceivable, then, that the middle portion of the string could be located infinitely far from us, thereby making the piece of string infinitely long, although we are holding both ends in our hands. Such a piece of string, of course, has A/Ω-infinity, just in case you were wondering.

It is probably easier to understand the operations of infinity (insofar as we are able to understand them at all) strictly within the context of mathematics, because we are used to working with infinity as a property of the sequence of numbers. But infinity can conceivably apply in other areas as well. Something might be thought of as infinitely large (Milissus' concept of the universe, for example), or infinitely powerful (the omnipotence of God), or infinitely heavy (perhaps the rock God makes that he is unable to lift), or infinitely dense (the concentration of all matter at a point just prior to the Big Bang, and sometimes unfairly applied to a student in his first philosophy course), or infinitely variable (the shapes of snowflakes) and so on. In the house of infinity, there are many mansions.

But our approach to these mansions must be by either first class or coach. In other words, there are two basic under-standings of infinity which should be recognized regardless of which area we intend to explore. Infinity may be understood as an actual or as a potential, and this distinction will prove to be of some significance when we finally get around to analyzing the concept of eternity. It is not really all that difficult to get at the distinction between an actual infinity and a potential infinity. Is there actually, for example, an infinite number of numbers? Or is it, rather, the case that, no matter which number we care to pick, there will always be that number plus one—i.e., there will always be a greater number? If one understands the infinity of the number system as an actual infinity, he will be inclined to believe that there are, in fact, infinitely many numbers. It will make sense to him to conceive that there actually might be an infinite number of particles in the universe, that we might even hold an infinite number of particles in our hand, since whatever object we pick up is infinitely subdivisible. This approach to infinity is what I meant by first class. It allows for an actual arrival at an infinite quantity.

On the other hand, one might understand infinity in quite a different way. We can understand the number system, for example, not as an actual but as a potential infinity. Here one might maintain that there is not, in fact, an infinite number of numbers, but rather that we will never find a number in the sequence of integers that is not followed by a greater number. In other words, for any number we care to pick, there will be a greater number. This means that, if we were to maintain that there is an infinite number of subdivisions in any given object, for example, we do not mean that there really (or actually) is an infinite number of entities in the object, but only that any given portion of that object can be divided again into two equal parts. This approach to infinity is what I meant by coach, since, unlike first class, we never quite arrive at the infinite. We are always on the way.

The mansions of infinity can be approached via first class or coach, but it does help if we understand which mode we have chosen. That is, we should keep in mind whether we are understanding infinity as an actual or as a potential. The mansions themselves will take on a somewhat different quality depending upon our choice. For example, if one were to maintain that God is omnipotent, that simply means that God is infinitely powerful. But if we are speaking of an actual infinite, then we would acknowledge the possibility of God actually exerting an infinite power in a given situation. If we mean a potential infinite, then we are committed only to the notion that, however much power God cares to exert in any given situation, he could exert more. That is, perhaps, a subtle distinction, but it is a distinction that makes a difference. Infinity can be understood as actual or potential, and this will have an effect on how we view its relationship to any given area.

We can now focus more specifically on how the concept of infinity relates to time. When we consider what is meant by "eternal," as in "eternal life," we immediately sense that there is a quality of infinity involved, and further, that it is in some way predicated of time. Just what sort of infinity is at work here? How, precisely, is it that infinity might modify time?

Time can be understood as infinite in any of the ways delineated above. Most people seem naturally to think of time as having what we have called Φ-infinity. That is, time has no beginning and no end. The present moment, like zero in the set Φ, is flanked by an infinite sequence of moments into the past and an infinite sequence of moments into the future. But this is not the only way time can be understood as infinite. If time is infinite, but not Φ-infinite, then it must have either a beginning or an end, or perhaps both. This is difficult to imagine, since we would be obliged to consider the possibility that time might somehow come into being or cease to be. It is, in fact, debatable whether time "exists" at all, or whether it is the product of human imagination. Time may be discovered or it may be invented. But either way, we should make some attempt to sharpen the concept. Does it make sense to think that time might have come into existence? If we imagine an empty universe (in mathematics it would be represented by a set containing no members at all—the null set), it is not easy to see how there would be any reality to time. Would time exist in an empty universe, without even a mind to experience duration? Obviously there would be nothing to measure time, but in what sense would there be time at all? Suppose, now, that the universe somehow became populated with the substance it now has. Certainly time would then become an appropriate concept. It is conceivable, then, that time might have A-infinity, having come into existence with the substance of the universe, thereby generating an infinite sequence of moments into the future. Again, it is at least conceivable that time might have Ω-infinity if we imagine that the universe, which has always existed, suddenly ceases to exist. The universe would resolve itself into the null set, and presumably this would entail the destruction of time itself. It is more difficult to understand how time might exhibit A/Ω-infinity, but this is also possible. If time has both a beginning and an end, there is not, in the usual sense, an infinite duration, but there nevertheless can be an infinite sequence of moments within any finite span of time. Just as there is an infinite number of fractions between zero and one, there is an infinite number of moments between 12:00 noon and 12:01 P.M.

In fact, it can be shown that between any two moments there is an infinite number of moments, so long as we assume that time is infinitely subdivisible. Time, then, might conceivably be infinite in any of these four ways.

How are we to understand the infinite quality of eternity? Can this analysis help us understand what is meant by eternal life? Well, it does seem to sharpen our sense of the options available. Probably most people would understand eternality as having Φ-infinity. That is, the initial reaction to a proposition like "x is eternal" is that x is an existing thing having no beginning or end. An eternal star, then, would be uncreated and indestructible, existing throughout an infinite past and confronting an infinite future. But when we speak of eternal life we mean to apply the predicate eternal not to a material subject, but to life itself and, more specifically, to our own individual souls. When eternality is predicated of the soul (or the mind), we might feel less inclined to understand this as Φ-infinity. There are those who believe that individual souls may indeed be temporally Φ-infinite, existing as uncreated, indestructible givens of reality. In fact, if the soul is understood as an indivisible and therefore indestructible substance, as Plato and Descartes believed, one might easily conclude that the soul is temporally Φ-infinite, as Plato did, although Descartes did not. It is not likely that such an essentially indestructible substance could be produced from any combination of matter and energy. Matter and energy are quantifiable and therefore divisible, at least in theory. But the soul is said to be indivisible. It cannot, then, be formed from a combination of ingredients since any combination might eventually be resolved into its component parts. If the soul does not come into existence through the interaction of matter and energy and if, further, the soul does exist as an indestructible substance, one just might conclude that the soul has always existed and will always continue to be. Thus, the soul's temporal status would be Φ-infinite. The obvious way out of this, and in fact the way chosen by Descartes and most Christian philosophers who accept a basically Platonic concept of the soul, is to maintain that the soul has come into being not through the interaction of the realm of matter and energy, but through the divine agency of God. The soul, then, would be understood as having been created at some point in time by God, subsequently to exist for eternity. The eternal quality possessed by such a soul would be A-infinity. It would have a beginning, but no end.

It is conceivable that a soul might be temporally Ω-infinite, although this does not readily strike us as a probable notion. The soul just might have existed from eternity until the present moment, only to be somehow annihilated. It would have no beginning in time, but it would have an end. But I can think of no good reason to take this possibility seriously, except that it is a possibility.

Might the eternality of the soul exhibit A/Ω-infinity? It might indeed. Since the soul is the seat of experience, it is certainly the case that our awareness of time is a function of the soul. It is the soul, or the mind, which allows us to experience the passage of time. Imagine now that the soul comes into being at a given moment in time, say T_1, and passes out of existence at some subsequent moment in time, say T_n. Our initial reaction to such a state of affairs might be that the soul would not be eternal. We are simply not used to thinking that an entity which comes into existence and then ceases to exist could be eternal in any reasonable way. Should we learn that such is the case with the soul we would naturally conclude that the soul does not possess eternal life and is therefore not immortal. But suppose we could increase the sensitivity of the soul in the following way. We all know that, whether or not there is any objective reality to time (that is, whether or not it would exist without minds to know it), there is certainly a subjective reality to time. We can and do experience longer and shorter periods of time. Sometimes this seems to bear little relationship to clock time. A rose may be a rose, but five minutes is not always five minutes. Five minutes spent reading a fascinating book like this may pass very quickly. Five minutes spent under water without any artificial breathing apparatus may seem virtually endless. Sometimes we notice the duration of a given period of time more than we do at other times. We can easily notice the individual seconds which make up each of the minutes in a span of five clock-time minutes. We can, if we direct our attention to it, notice much shorter durations of time, e.g., a half second, a quarter of a second, and even shorter than that.

Imagine, however, that our awareness is so intensified that we could notice our experience of one one-hundredth of a second. That may not be possible, but it is at least conceivable. Imagine, now, that our capacity of awareness is intensified to the point where we can notice each moment in time. If time is infinitely subdivisible, then we would experience an infinite sequence of moments between any two moments of clock time. Thus, a soul which comes into being at time T_1 and ceases to exist at a subsequent moment, T_n, just might be said to be eternal if it can experience time as A/Ω-infinite. The fact that we do not experience each moment in time does not at all entail that we cannot. If a soul is given, or develops, the capacity to experience eternity in the interval between any two moments, it would be arbitrary to say that such a soul is not immortal. The important quality of eternity in the concept of eternal life is certainly related to infinity as it applies to time. Since any finite period of time is infinitely subdivisible there is an eternal quality in all such periods of time. If, further, the soul should attain to the ability to experience eternality as A/Ω-infinite, what greater satisfaction could be desired? Is there something inherently more desirable in the concept of eternity as A-infinite, or Φ-infinite?

It is, after all, the experience of eternity that we seek. It simply makes no sense to desire an eternity that cannot be experienced. Is it possible to experience eternity as A-infinite? Can experience conceivably embrace an endless duration, an infinite sequence of moments into the future?

The point here is that we may be making a mistake in attempting to understand eternal life as endless clock-time duration projecting into the future. Infinity can be understood as an expansion or as a division. Time may expand infinitely into the past and/or the future. It may also be infinitely subdivided into the present. But we can experience only the present. It seems curiously fashionable today to deny the reality of the present. I have had many discussions with students who maintain that time is only the future becoming the past. They believe that the notion of the present is only a reference to the interface between past and future. "There is no now," said one of my students in a poem she wrote about time. Yet this idea is surely mistaken. There is only now. We cannot experience the future, except as a present anticipation. This will not change even if we should develop the capacity to travel through time. We would still experience only the now, or more precisely, *our* now. The present is the only time we have, and all we can ever have. It is true that any given moment quickly slips somehow into the past before we can quite catch hold of it. But that does not mean that the *now* slips into the past. Nor does it mean that there is no now. There is always now. There is only now. Our experience is always a present experience, even if it is an experience of a past memory or a future anticipation.

Theologians sometimes say that all time is as the present to the Lord. And this just might make some sense. If it is possible to experience eternity, it must be in the present moment. But if eternity is experienced in the present moment, it seems it must be via an intensification of awareness such that the eternal quality of that moment can be sensed. The infinite subdivisibility of time would guarantee that there is an A/Ω-eternity within any given span of time. It is there to be experienced by any soul capable of noticing it. Generally, we take no notice of the passage of five minutes of time. But if we direct our attention to it, we can notice each of the seconds which make up any five minutes of time. By intensifying our awareness we can actually experience durations of time as short as one-tenth of a second or even shorter. What are the theoretical limits to our capacity to experience time? Our analysis of ego death indicated that it may be possible to experience a transcendence of all limits, even if it is at the cost of the ego itself. Would it not be arbitrary to place any limits on the possibility of experiencing time, especially in view of the contemporary research into the nature of consciousness which hints at some startling qualities of certain altered states of consciousness?

Precisely this analysis is suggested by the concept of ego death. It can be argued, and has been, that the experience of ego death is an experience of eternity as a kind of timeless now. Because ego death involves the absence of any sort of plurality, the sense of time as past, present, and future would be unavailable. The experience would have to be one of total now-ness. Since those who experience ego death often claim to have experienced eternity, perhaps this is an experience of time as A/Ω-infinite. It cannot be an experience of an endless sequence of moments, either from the past or into the future, since this would involve plurality. We are left with the likelihood that, if eternity is indeed experienced in ego death, it is an experience of time as A/Ω-infinite.

Reflecting on our distinction between an actual and a potential infinite, how are we to understand eternity? It is probably fair to say that, in terms of ultimate satisfaction, the experience of eternity as an actual rather than a potential infinite would be more fulfilling. In fact, that almost sounds like a tautology. Actual infinites have a completeness about them, while potential infinites are open-ended. If eternity, as applied to the soul, exhibits A-infinity, for example, it would seem reasonable to suppose that such a quality must be experienced as a potential rather than an actual infinite. The soul would come into being at a moment in time to endure an endless succession of moments into the future, a sequence which could never be completed and therefore could never completely be experienced. The soul would experience unending duration, but so far that is exactly what all of us have experienced in this life. There would simply be more of the same. If I were allowed to vote on the metaphysical nature of the soul I would hesitate to vote for an eternity that was A-infinite, although this is exactly how the concept of eternal life is generally understood. The nature of metaphysics does not, of course, depend upon my vote, but the prospect of my soul being temporally A-infinite is unsatisfying in at least two respects. First, it could never allow for an actual experience of eternity. The infinite would forever stretch out beyond the actual experience. And second, it does not differ in any genuinely interesting way from the normal experience of life as we know it. Now my experience in this life has been, on the whole, definitely upbeat. I do not dislike this life, nor do I regret it in any way whatsoever. But I should hope that eternity would take on a different quality. I do not look for more of the same. More of the same could never allow for the possibility of completion or fulfillment. I would be approaching eternity by coach, as a potential, never quite arriving, always on the way. And while it is doubtless true that enjoyment can be found in the pursuit of truth, the satisfaction of discovery remains the final goal. A metaphysical system in which eternity is A-infinite condemns all of us to being perpetual seekers. It further suggests an eternal alienation from that which we seek, and therefore an endless frustration.

We might be tempted to believe that we could never actually experience an open-ended infinity. As long as the sequence of moments is uncompleted, any experience of infinity must be potential rather than actual. But this is not quite the case. If the soul is temporally Φ-infinite, for example, that would seem to entail that an infinite sequence of moments in the past has actually been experienced, although the sequence of moments to come must be sensed as a potential. But objections similar to those raised with the notion of A-infinity can be noted here. There remains an ultimate incompleteness to eternity. Even though the soul would, on this analysis, have survived an infinite sequence of past moments, and therefore, in a sense, would have experienced eternity, there remains the endless quest into the future. The soul continues to wander, like the Ancient Mariner, in search of that which it cannot possess. Alienation, frustration, incompleteness—these are as much the final marks of the soul which is Φ-infinite as of the soul which is temporally A-infinite.

The possibility that the temporal quality of the soul may be Ω-infinite is troublesome at this point. I have already dismissed this option as highly unlikely, since it involves the notion that the soul has existed from past eternity to the present, only to face annihilation. While acknowledging that this is logically possible, there being no obvious contradiction in the concept, the possibility that the soul may be temporally Ω-infinite is surely remote. There is simply no good reason to suppose that this option is the case. But if it were, it would, like our analysis of Φ-infinity, suggest the possibility of an experience of an actual, open-ended infinite—in this case reaching into the past. The experience, unlike that associated with A-infinity, would be complete with the moment of annihilation, and would presumably include awareness of the unending sequence of moments into the past, as was the case with Φ-infinity. The mere statement that there is no good reason to take this option seriously, of course, is hardly conclusive. But it is difficult to understand the rationale of a metaphysical model in which souls, having survived an infinite period of time into the past, suffer annihilation.

The possibility that the soul might be temporally A/Ω-infinite is tantalizing. The total experience of the soul would have a beginning and an end. The experience would therefore be completed and ultimately actualized rather than remaining forever potential. But the quality of experience for a soul whose eternality is A/Ω-infinite would include an actual experience of eternity. Eternity would be experienced as a completed whole, with a beginning and an end, and yet it would be infinite. It would be an actual infinite, an infinite which might be possessed.

Well, what is our verdict? Of course we cannot demonstrate conclusively that the soul is or is not immortal, and no pretense at this point is being made. We cannot, therefore, know whether the soul is temporally Φ-infinite, A-infinite, Ω-infinite, A/Ω-infinite, or none of the above. But we are not required to conclude that the issue is absolutely inscrutable. There is some evidence available. There are hints here and there. While acknowledging the definite possibility that we may be wrong, we are surely entitled to make an informed guess as to the nature and destiny of our souls.

The prima facie case seems to favor a negative judgment about our prospects for surviving the grave. Our knowledge of another person's soul is normally gained indirectly. We do not experience his mind, but come to know his mind by observing his physical behavior. His death brings an end to his physical behavior and, therefore, an end to the only means by which we were able to know his mind. It is natural to conclude, in the absence of any evidence to the contrary, that the mind expires with the death of the body. But it is important to note that this is not a logical deduction. We have maintained throughout this book that the mind, whatever it is, is not adequately identified as physical substance. If the body is defined as a Cartesian extended substance, then the mind is not identical with the body. The mind may or may not be completely dependent upon the body, but our subjective, mental experience is simply not identical with objective, material substance. This means that there is no logical connection between the status of the mind and the status of the body, and that it is at least logically possible for the mind to exist without the body. But it is logically possible that the moon is made out of baloney. The fact that any given proposition does not contradict itself is no assurance that it is true. Nor can that fact even count as evidence in favor of the proposition.

But some philosophers are not even willing to grant that disembodied survival of the grave is a sensible concept. Antony Flew, for example, compares the suggestion that a person might survive the destruction of his body to the possibility that "a nation might outlast the annihilation of all its members."[2] Those who reason along this line are understanding the concept of a person in terms of the physical body we encounter, and there is strong support for this. What, after all, is left of what we know about a person once we have subtracted all the physical presentations he provides us? I do come to know another person by encountering his physical presence, watching his physical behavior, and observing his physical responses to me and his environment. My knowledge of him comes via one or more of the five senses, and these do seem to depend upon his physical existence. Once that physical mode is taken away, I can gain no further knowledge of him. On this analysis it certainly does make sense to suspect that the concept of a person surviving the destruction of his physical body is quite irrational.

But the fact that I come to know other persons by encountering their physical presence does not at all imply that the concept of a person must refer precisely to his physical substance. If that were the case, then when viewing a cadaver we should not be inclined to feel that the person has "gone." The physical substance is still there. But that is simply ridiculous. Even in the presence of the body, we sense very deeply that the *person* is missing. Nor can we equate our understanding of person, or self, with the motions of the body—i.e., the sequence of physical behavior patterns that we observe in another person. No artificial inducement of motion in a dead body could possibly reassure us that the person we once knew was now present with us. The source of the confusion here, it seems to me, is that we forget that our concept of person, or self, is based not at all on our observation of other people, but rather on our subjective experience of ourselves. If someone were to suggest to me that my understanding of what it means to be a self is derived from the observations I have made of other people, my initial reaction would be that he could not possibly be serious. It should be obvious that I have a far better source of information available to me than mere observation of external objects I call "persons." I can, and do, have direct and immediate experience of a person—myself. I may, of course, gain some information about myself in exactly the same way I come to know other persons. I can look at myself in a mirror, listen to myself sing in the shower, and so on. I can, as subject, observe myself, as object. I can learn things about myself the way I must learn things about others—by using one or more of the five senses.

But, unlike the case with other persons, my knowledge of myself is not restricted to the avenue of the five senses.

Obviously it is not. There is clearly a "sixth sense," although it has no unusual or occult quality about it. Awareness, or consciousness, as I experience it, has a reflexive quality. I can be directly aware of my own awareness. I can sense myself without making any use of the five senses, and this sixth sense is a genuine and legitimate source of knowledge. It is how I come to know myself. I have a direct experience of myself, and it is from that that I derive my concept of what a person is. My understanding of the self is grounded, not in my observation of other persons, but in the far more adequate experience of my own consciousness. My knowledge of other persons is indeed along the lines Flew has suggested. I depend upon their physical presentation to me. What I know about them does depend upon the sense data produced by their presence in physical form. But it is simply a mistake to conclude from this that I construct a concept of person on such limited experience as this. I stand in a subject-object relationship to other persons, and therefore I am necessarily separated from them. My knowledge of them is indirect and limited. But I am not separated from myself. Within me there is no subject-object distinction. My knowledge of myself is direct and immediate. Since I am a person, and since I can know myself in this very special and superior way, my concept of person has its roots in my understanding of myself.

Now it can be shown that the physical mode is not a logical or rational necessity in my understanding of the self. While it is true that I can observe, via the five senses, my physical self, it is also true that I can sense myself without resorting to any of the five senses. The experience of my own mind is clearly possible without using my eyes, my ears, my nose, my tongue, or my fingers. I do not even have to think of my physical body when thinking about myself. In fact this is usually the case. During periods of introspection I do not find that I am thinking about my body as seen in a mirror or by others. I have no thought whatsoever of the way my hair is combed and parted, the clothes I am wearing, the spatial dimensions I fill, or anything else of the sort. I reflect directly upon my emotions, my hopes, my fears, my confusions, or whatever. Perhaps I cannot do this without my body. But I can certainly do it without thinking about my body, and this is precisely where Flew is wrong. The most important things about myself simply have nothing to do with the material substance encountered by other people. And I frankly assume that the most important things about other people have nothing to do with their material substance which I encounter. My concept of a person is based upon my best estimate of his emotional matrix. It is his subjective nature that interests me, even though it is true that my knowledge of his subjective nature depends upon his objective presence. My concept of a person, then, can indeed be separated from my concept of a physical object. I simply do not equate "me" with my physical body. I can imagine, then, the possibility that I might somehow survive in the absence of that body. At least I deny the contention that such a concept is conceptually absurd.

The issue, then, rests fundamentally upon the metaphysical status of the mind. We simply do not know whether the mind can exist without the body. It is conceivable that there might be thought and subjective experience apart from the objective material substance of the body. But we cannot know whether such things in fact happen until we understand better the nature of mind. Whether mental experience is "substantial" enough to survive in the absence of physical substance depends upon further analysis of the nature of mind, perhaps in conjunction with research along lines similar to those suggested in chapter 6. But we do not need to wait upon such discoveries in order to engage in some speculation. Philosophy lends itself to a consideration of areas in which our knowledge is relatively meager. There are hints and bits of evidence that we might notice. Perhaps we can make an educated guess. We cannot do any worse than be wrong. And we might just be right.

Although we have noted that the prima facie case is against survival, it should be pointed out that this case rests, not upon positive evidence against survival, but rather upon the lack of evidence for survival. (We have rejected the claim that survival of death is a logical absurdity.) I have never encountered a ghost, and I am not convinced that anyone else has either. But what is it, after all, that I *do* encounter? I encounter just exactly what Antony Flew means by a person—i.e., his physical body, or more precisely, my *ideas* of his physical body. I have never encountered another person's mind. The death of that body seems to entail the end of my encounter with that person. If there is a mode of survival beyond the grave, it is surely mental in nature. Since I am unable to experience another person's mind, I should not wonder that the death of his body terminates my experience of him, whether or not he has survived the grave. The lack of such experience, then, would seem to be precisely what we should expect, regardless of whether or not the soul is immortal. This does not argue for immortality, but only against the prima facie case against survival. The prima facie case is impotent, since it is quite compatible with beliefs for and against immortality. But that prima facie case—that is, the lack of further knowledge or experience of those who die—is the heart of the case against immortality. If it is powerless, as we have suggested, then we are at a standoff, unless we can begin to construct another argument one way or the other. Let us do so.

I am not sure how to go about building an argument directly against immortality, other than to point out our lack of experience of the dead person, or somehow to show that the concept is inherently inconsistent. But neither of these options is persuasive for reasons already cited. Perhaps the picture might be clarified if we examine the evidence for survival. Of course we must ground any argument for immortality in experience of some kind, since we can never know anything apart from experience. Now we seem to be required to look for an experience of death. We have already noted that it is possible to experience dying. But the issue is whether we can experience death itself. If that is possible, then survival of death is a viable option. If death is the termination of experience, then there is no survival. Our discussion of ego death in the previous chapter is relevant here. There are many reports from people who have experienced ego death which indicate that they consider it an experience of death itself. They may very well be wrong in that interpretation, since they are comparing the experience of ego death to an experience of which they are, presumably, ignorant. But they may be correct, too. The experience of ego death is a possible source of information about what happens in death. If my ego is defined by its limits, by those qualities which set it apart from other things, then the negation of those limits certainly appears to entail the negation of the ego itself. A triangle, for example, is defined as a three-sided figure. It is limited by its three sides, but those three sides set it apart from other things and make it what it is. Negating its three-sidedness negates the triangle itself. It is reasonable to suppose that the limits of my ego, which define me as an identifiable entity, are a function of the physical mode through which the ego is expressed. I am here rather than there because my physical body has spatial location. I am now rather than then, again because my physical body exists within time. I see this rather than that because of the limitations of sight, and so on. The death of my body may mean the negation of those limiting (or differentiating) qualities. This suggests that my ego is *not* immortal, since that which defines it will be negated at death. But what we know about ego death further suggests that awareness may continue even in the absence of the ego. Death may very well mean the end of the individual self as separated from other entities. The limits of awareness which define the ego may be negated. The ego is then negated. But is awareness itself necessarily negated? Not unless we can show that awareness is necessarily limited. The negation of the limitations of awareness would then entail the negation of awareness itself. But it is not easy to see how we might demonstrate that awareness is necessarily limited, or why we should be inclined to think that it is. A drop of water is defined by its shape, which separates it from all other things. It is quite literally destroyed, as a drop, when it is placed in the ocean. But the water itself is not destroyed. Only the surface tension which once defined a specific quantity of water is gone. This effectively destroys the drop as an identifiable entity, but obviously that which was limited, i.e., the substance itself, is not annihilated. What was once a drop of water is now dispersed into the whole.

Perhaps this is analogous to ego death. Mental substance, whatever it is, may be defined, or limited, by the biophysical mode through which it is expressed, just as the drop of water is defined, or limited, by the surface tension which gives it shape. After all, we do seem to be separated from everything else precisely because of our physical location in space and time. The destruction, or death, of the body might just be the negation of the ''surface tension'' of a certain quantum of mental substance. But since that is exactly what defines my ego, thereby making me ''me,'' rather than anything or everything else, I am led to the conclusion that my ego is not immortal after all. I am interested in whether or not I survive death, and this analysis suggests that I do not. In attempting to construct an argument for immortality based upon a plausible concept of the ego I have, in fact, developed an analysis which indicates that the immortality of my soul is an illusion. And this really sounds much like what Antony Flew was suggesting when he defined persons as the physical objects we encounter. The destruction of that physical object entails the destruction of that person. I rejected his analysis of what is meant by the concept of person, and I continue to do so. But I must recognize now that his analysis makes a valid point. Certainly the biodegradeable physical substance of an individual is not entirely irrelevant to my concept of him as a person. When I think of another individual, I do think of his physical appearance. But when I think of myself, I tend not to do so. What is the source of the tension here? It is partly due to the fact that my knowledge of another person is dependent upon my experience of him as a physical being and therefore in thinking about him I refer to his physical appearance. Since I cannot know directly his subjective thoughts and feelings, which are available to him alone, I cannot use them directly as part of my concept of him. I can only guess at what they may be, from what I have seen in terms of his physical appearance and behavior. But since I have direct access to my own subjective nature, it is unnecessary for me to think of myself as an objective physical body. And this is why I reject Flew's analysis of the concept of a person. When it comes to the best source of knowledge available to me concerning what a person is, namely myself, his analysis seems incorrect, or at least incomplete. But if the death of the physical body produces an annihilation of the ego, as I have suggested, in what significant way does my answer to the question of immortality differ from Flew's?

There is, in logic, an axiom known as the law of Excluded Middle. This law simply says that any proposition must either be true or be false, that between affirmation and denial there is no middle ground. Most people think of the question of immortality along similar lines. Either we survive death or we do not. If we do, then I, as an identifiable individual self, will continue to have experiences beyond the grave. If we do not, then I am lost.

My destiny is a great big zip, an ontological zero. Surely there can be no middle ground, no compromise, between affirmation and denial in this question. Well, I am suggesting that there might be. It does not appear to be reasonable to look for the survival of my ego beyond death. At least I can find no plausible analysis which would lead me in that direction. But the implications of this stand are not entirely negative. Just as I insist, on what to me is irrefutable evidence, that there is more to me as a person than my biological substance, there may also be more to me than my precious ego. If *my* awareness, that is, my ego, is the result of a limitation of conscious substance, possibly as a consequence of the physical medium through which it is expressed, then the death of my ego may yield, not the absence of awareness, but the absence of a *limited* awareness, which is what defined the ego in the first place. Perhaps death would annihilate the ego, not in favor of absolute nothingness, but in favor of absolute everythingness. It may be that death releases mental substance from the bondage of the ego in favor of a mode of awareness something like what Canadian psychiatrist R. M. Bucke called cosmic consciousness. And the possibilities here are genuinely exciting, even if we cannot look forward to a continuation of the ego. This is a sort of middle ground. A denial of the immortality of the ego may not entail the denial of the immortal nature of awareness itself. If ego-awareness is limited awareness, then perhaps the reverse is true—i.e., limited awareness may be what is meant by the ego. If so, then the negation of the ego may only be the negation of the limitation. I am not immortal. I do not expect to survive death. But perhaps the ultimate reality of my ego is awareness itself, unlimited, undefined, and undifferentiated. We have suggested, in chapter 6, that death will bring a reconciliation of what we are with the ultimate reality in which we are grounded. If this analysis is plausible, then it is likely that we, like the drop of water tossed into the ocean, are doomed in terms of our identity in the ego. But, as the drop of water loses only its "drop-ness" and not its "water-ness," it just may be that we, like drops of awareness, will lose only our ego and not the substance which was limited by the ego.

The question of immortality, then, should really be asked in two different ways: (1) Will our awareness survive death? The most reasonable answer seems to be no. (2) Will awareness itself survive death? The answer suggested here is yes. And we are referring not to the awareness of other surviving egos, but to awareness itself, in which all egos are grounded. If our mental substance is somehow formed through a bracketing of an oceanic mental substance, then the negation of that bracketing entails the destruction of our egos. Death does not entirely lose its sting. We are, after all, somewhat attached to ourselves and we cannot easily accept the loss of the ego. But death is not necessarily victorious either. There seems to be no good reason to suppose that the ego is the ultimate reality of ourselves. Perhaps death will free us from the limitations of ourselves and allow an experience of the very ground of our being.

It would be helpful if we could somehow suggest a clearer picture of what that experience might be like, but we are rapidly getting in beyond our depth. There are claims and counterclaims about the nature of cosmic consciousness, and we are really not equipped to evaluate them. But let us turn our attention to one facet of the experience and let it go at that. We noted earlier in the chapter that the question of immortality involved an analysis of the infinity of time. By denying the immortality of the ego we have denied the possibility that the ego will experience eternality in any of the ways mentioned. That is, the ego will not experience an endless duration of time, either potential or actual. It will not, therefore, experience time as Φ-infinite or A-infinite or Ω-infinite or A/Ω-infinite. But if awareness itself is eternal, then we might be able to analyze the mode of infinity at another level. We have already noted that it is unlikely that cosmic consciousness would lend itself to an experience of time as any kind of sequence of moments. That would involve at least the separation of time into past, present, and future, and we have seen that the experience of ego death does not seem to involve any sort of plurality. This is why it was suggested that cosmic consciousness could be an experience of eternality as A/ Ω-infinite. If there are no limitations on awareness, then perhaps eternality can be experienced within a given moment.

This is exactly what is suggested by many of the writings of those who claim to have experienced cosmic consciousness. R. M. Bucke, for example, in writing of his experience, makes the following statement: "I became conscious in myself of eternal life. It was not a conviction that I would have eternal life, but a consciousness that I possessed eternal life then." [3] This conviction did not depend upon the sense of having passed through an infinite sequence of moments, either from the past or into the future. It seems to spring from an awareness of eternality within what to an outsider would appear to be a temporally finite experience. Bucke himself notes that the vision lasted only "a few seconds and was gone." It does not seem to occur to him that there is any contradiction involved in the experience of eternality within such a short span of time. If there is any validity to his experience, it certainly suggests that the mode of eternality is A/Ω-infinite. Further, he clearly means to assert that the experience of eternality was the experience of an actual, not a potential, infinite. It had nothing to do with a belief that he *would* experience eternal life. He claims to have been aware of possessing eternal life within the moment of his experience. If cosmic consciousness involves the loss of the limitations upon consciousness, perhaps awareness is indeed capable of experiencing the eternal quality locked into each moment of time.

All this indicates that death might possibly be a rather fascinating prospect, even though we may note with some regret the loss of our ego. It may be that a proper perspective on the nature of the ego will reveal to us that it is just inappropriate to view it as the most important entity in the cosmos. Entirely new and significant vistas of experience may attend the death of the ego. The truth may turn out to be the most satisfying of all the possible prospects. We may be heading for an experience of eternity which brings us to infinity first class. The possibility that death will allow an experience of eternal life as an actual rather than a potential excites the imagination.

One obvious, and appropriate, objection to this analysis is that it seems grounded in the assumption that the quality of the experience of cosmic consciousness known as ego death is a preview of some sort to an eventual experience of death itself. It is clearly a matter of conjecture to make such an assumption. The death of the body may produce nothing remotely similar to an experience of ego death. Those reports from people who have almost died which indicate that they experienced a basically mystical consciousness during their brush with death are certainly far from conclusive. Death itself may still be the end, not only of the ego, but of any and all possibility of consciousness in any form whatsoever. There is no argument available which will convincingly demonstrate the connection between the experience of ego death and the event of death itself. Lacking a substantial reason for making that connection, our speculations in this area apparently become nothing more than sophisticated mythologies, reflecting at best psychological facts about our deepest desires while revealing nothing of metaphysical truths.

There is frankly no good way to avoid the real thrust of this objection, which suggests that our reasoning is finally built upon a hunch and very little more. That is, in fact, basically an accurate assessment of our position. It seems to come down to something like a guess based upon a wet finger held in the air. While granting that the odds are probably against this analysis being correct, I can only observe that the odds seem even heavier against any other analysis I can think of. The final truth about the nature of ultimate reality and our final reconciliation with it may be quite unlike anything yet thought of in metaphysical speculation. But we must begin where we are and work toward the truth with what we have. We have reason, and we have feeling. We should work toward a metaphysical analysis of death that is consistent with itself and with whatever known facts there may be. But it is just ridiculous to suppose that we can do that while ignoring the most obvious of all facts—our own subjective awareness, by which and through which we know all other facts. No adequate metaphysics of death can avoid coming to some conclusions about the nature of mind. For here is the real issue. Furthermore, any analysis which dismisses the mind as a myth or a category mistake or an insignificance is itself to be dismissed, no matter how logical it seems. The structures and categories of logic must not be rejected. Without them we are helpless before competing claims. The very concept of truth rests upon the logical structure which distinguishes it from error. But logical structures alone are vacuous. Of and by themselves they are absolutely devoid of any content. They lack substance. Knowing that *a* thing is identical with itself tells us nothing about *the* thing of which that is true. Logic assures us that any given proposition must be either true or false and not both, but it does not tell us which propositions are worth considering. The focus of our attention, the very direction of our interests, cannot be a function of logic.

We simply cannot deduce from logical axioms the metaphysical areas we wish to explore. We cannot gain our initial hypotheses about the nature of reality from the axioms themselves. A proposition must be either true or false, but which proposition shall we consider first, and is *it* true?

We are forced always to begin with ourselves. We must, like Descartes, begin with the absolutely inescapable demands of the ego itself and work from there. Here is the source of our interests, and here is where we must begin. What is it that we wish to know? In which areas shall we pursue truth? The answers to these questions are not to be found at the end of a syllogism. Logic is like a road map. It can keep us from getting lost, so long as we know where it is that we want to go. But no road map can tell us where we want to go. It can only show us the many places we can go. Once we have chosen our destination, it will show us the direction. Logic can keep us from getting lost as we pick our way through the wilderness of our own ignorance. But that wilderness is vast indeed. We cannot simply decide to explore it all at once. We have to make a clearing in that wilderness one tree at a time. This book has chosen to explore a very dark wilderness, the darkness of death itself. That decision was not dictated by logic. The structure of logic may be vacuous, but it will completely and absolutely destroy any metaphysical system which violates it.

The analysis of the issue of immortality as we have developed it may be very wide of the mark. There is no claim whatsoever to the effect that it is possible to demonstrate conclusively the validity of our analysis with our present state of knowledge. We have given a specific focus to the question of immortality and have ignored the more traditional arguments in this area. This is because the traditional arguments for and against immortality are based upon a limited concept of personal immortality which appears to ignore the broader possibilities of an ego-less

164

experience. The question of the survival of the personal ego does not exhaust the issue of immortality. Our approach to this issue may not be correct. But it seems to be internally consistent. It does not, so far as I can determine, conflict with anything else I know to be the case. And it begins to provide a framework within which a great many fragmented bits and pieces of knowledge might begin to fit in a consistent and coherent whole. It has the ring of truth, although admittedly the sound is more like the ping of my typewriter bell than the sonorous authority of Big Ben. At the very least, this analysis may prove to be an irritant around which a pearl of genuine wisdom may develop.

CHAPTER 9
Confronting Death

Since we have wandered for sometime in the realms of metaphysical speculations about death, it is perhaps appropriate to conclude this book on a more "realistic" note. This is not to suggest that we were being entirely unrealistic in our previous considerations. But there comes a point when we begin to wonder, not so much what *the* truth about death is, but what it all means to me, a far more personal question. We have assumed that the pursuit of death is important, not simply as one fascinating topic among many, but also because it is a deeply significant event we must all confront. Most people have a vague feeling that there are better and worse ways of facing death, but have not been able to penetrate the issue much beyond that. We shall present in this chapter the basic attitudes toward death and consider whether everyone should confront death in the same way. In other words, are certain attitudes toward death really better than, or more appropriate than, others? Finally, we shall consider the significance of one's attitude toward death in determining the basic quality of his life.

In dealing with the metaphysics of death we should never forget that death is finally a very personal thing. In spite of certain theological formulations, it is not possible for anyone to die for us. We must do our own dying. We may avoid an intellectual analysis of death as a metaphysical event, but we cannot forever put off coming to terms with death as a personal event. In determining how we should confront death, we may find it useful to identify certain basic attitudes toward death which have been held by various people. It is certainly true that there are as many different attitudes in this area as there are individuals who have them. Yet it is not difficult to see that these may be grouped generally under three headings.

Geoffrey Gorer, a British social anthropologist, has written an essay entitled "The Pornography of Death." The title indicates one of the basic attitudes taken by many people toward death. Death is sometimes felt to be a kind of obscenity, utterly without redeeming social value. Those whose orientation toward death is along this line tend to avoid any confrontation with the issue, believing that it is not a topic to be considered by decent people. In developing seminars in the philosophy of death, I have encountered this attitude in several people, who indicated that any interest in this area must be some sort of morbid perversion. It is certainly true that there are perverted interests in death, but the assumption that all attention to this topic is some kind of variation on the theme of necrophilia is clearly unwarranted. It is more likely that those who view death as a form of pornography, a filth to be avoided by any clean-minded individual, are themselves guilty of perversion. Death is the final scene in the drama of our individual existence. We shall all, every one of us, play it out. And we shall do so in complete ignorance, or on the basis of an understanding which we have worked out during our lives. It is difficult to see how we can have any moral obligation to remain ignorant in this area. Further, to view death as pornography is to make a very unwarranted assumption about ourselves as individuals, an assumption which itself borders on perversion. It is that we are entities whose origin and destiny are basically evil and unworthy of decent interest. Those who attempt to avoid coming to terms with death on this line of reasoning exhibit a deep feeling, echoing the words of e.e. cummings: "forgive us,o life!the sin of Death." [1] Perhaps I am

167

mistaken, but it seems to me that such a view is itself obviously indecent and therefore unworthy of our further consideration.

Assuming, then, that death legitimately demands our attention, we can identify two general attitudes toward death which have been taken by many people. The first one we shall consider is well expressed in a poem by Dylan Thomas, the first portion of which reads:

> Do not go gentle into that good night,
> Old age should burn and rave at close of day;
> Rage, rage against the dying of the light.[2]

Certainly the inevitability of death does not entail that we should welcome it. It may be futile to resist, but resistance in the face of an evil, no matter how overpowering it may be, can lift an individual to new heights of dignity. There is no perversion here. There is instead, a ringing NO! hurled against the cosmos itself. One need not entertain any false hopes about the prospects of success in battle against death. It is a matter of integrity. If death is viewed as an evil, then we degrade ourselves by welcoming it. A similar attitude is expressed by Edna St. Vincent Millay, in her poem "Dirge Without Music," which concludes with these words:

> Down, down, down into the darkness of the grave
> Gently they go, the beautiful, the tender, the kind;
> Quietly they go, the intelligent, the witty, the brave.
> I know. But I do not approve. And I am not resigned.[3]

There is rebellion in this attitude which, in spite of its futility, speaks of dignity. It is predicated upon the assumption that death is an evil. It is not difficult to understand the basis for such a belief. Death is the ultimate threat, the final negation of our possibilities, the defeat of our hopes for an abiding significance. It does something to the very quality of life itself. Death forces us to see ourselves in the context of eternity, and the vision is not particularly encouraging. We live as though it were important that we live one way rather than another. Our lives are driven by a deep sense that it makes a difference whether we succeed or not. We are motivated by our hopes which attract us and our fears which repel us, and we naturally desire the experience of completion, fruition, of the self. Death guarantees not only that we shall fail, but also that it will ultimately make no difference. Which of us knows, or cares, whether a distant ancestor was a good or a foul individual? Of course that consideration was important to him, but he is long gone and forgotten. Even his memory has been swallowed up in the relatively short duration of time between his death and the present moment. Did he succeed? Was he gentle with his wife? Was he a good father? Was he a thief? We just do not know, and simply cannot be moved to try and find out. The end result of his life, therefore, is the same, no matter how these questions are answered. He is forgotten. And we ourselves face the same prospect. We are subject to the same process. We too shall be forgotten.

Death seems to make our lives pointless and futile. It is the final absurdity of a life which began in absurdity. Jean-Paul Sartre, in his epic work, *Being and Nothingness,* makes exactly this point: "It is absurd that we are born; it is absurd that we die." Because death seems to ensure that our individual existence can have no eternal significance, we are forced to confront a destiny which makes our strivings absurd. Sartre writes, "Death is . . . that which on principle removes all meaning from life." Such considerations have led many philosophers to suggest that the appropriate attitude toward death is rebellion. The inevitability of death is no reason to grant it our approval. If death is an evil, it is not to be welcomed. We do, after all, have the possibility of integrity. And integrity demands that we resist whatever threatens to degrade that which is valuable and good. If we cannot believe that our hopes and our potentialities are valuable and good, then we are already degraded and our cause is utterly absurd. Rebellion against death allows us to cultivate the only thing we really have—our dignity. This view is reflected in a statement made by Jacqueline Susann, a popular contemporary writer. "I have no intention of aging gracefully," she wrote. "I will go out kicking, screaming, fighting the battle of eternal youth." Miss Susann made that statement knowing that she had terminal cancer. The cancer was ultimately victorious, but does that negate the dignity of the manner in which Miss Susann faced death? There is no illusion, no deception in this attitude. There is no pretense that the battle with death will be successful. It is the decision that individual integrity requires resistance, even against an omnipotent evil.

But *is* death an evil? Some philosophers have thought that individual integrity entails that death be welcomed. "To philosophize is to learn how to die," wrote Karl Jaspers in *The Way to Wisdom,* a contemporary echo of the Socratic pronouncement from which the title of this book is taken.[4] Another German philosopher, Martin Heidegger, makes a similar point in his work *Being and Time.* We cannot really be free in life unless its negation in death is recognized and embraced fully. Those who accept this orientation toward death do not believe that death is a thing to be feared or contended with. We must learn to come to terms with death; we must live in order to settle our accounts with death. Many philosophers who have advanced this view of death understand death, not as a tragedy, nor even as the ground of absurdity, but as the very fulfillment of our existence. It is the final resolution of our struggles in life. Life is a process of becoming. It is in motion and therefore cannot itself be understood as complete. That toward which life moves is death. The distinction between life and death may be understood as the difference between

170

becoming and being. Life, by its very definition in our individual existences, is always becoming. Its basic quality is potential, not actual. As long as the process is in motion, it is incomplete. But as long as we are alive, the process of life is in motion. It is possible to understand death as a final resolution of the process of life. Death may be seen as our ultimate absorption in being, the only escape from the incompleteness of becoming. It is not easy to feel the power of this position unless one is already philosophically inclined. We find it difficult to see ourselves against the backdrop of the eternal. Death seems to guarantee incompleteness. It appears to ensure that our potentialities will never be actualized. We naturally associate being with our individual existence, and nonbeing with death. There are no possibilities, no processes, no anythings in nonbeing. To be is to live. Whatever "is-ness" we possess is felt to be in life, and that is negated in death. It takes a philosopher to twist our common-sense view into the notion that life, as potential and becoming, is in fact the negation of death, which is fully actualized being. Our analysis of immortality in the previous chapter may please a mathematician or a philosopher, but *I* am still doomed. The negation of my ego might be philosophically satisfying, but it remains psychologically frightening.

> Your fear of death is but the trembling
> of the shepherd when he stands before the
> king whose hand is to be laid upon him in
> honor.[5]

So says the prophet, through whom Kahlil Gibran presents his philosophy. But we are still frightened. We tremble, for we are neither prophets nor poets, nor even very good philosophers. Yet we must face death with them. The question becomes, not how should we face death, but how *can* we face death? What are our capabilities?

The question now is whether we can separate ourselves from the notion that our individual egos are cosmically important. If we cannot, then death is truly to be feared since it threatens the survival of our egos and therefore claims a victory over that which is ultimately important to us. But if we can work toward a broader perspective, if we can cultivate a concept of ourselves in the context of ultimate reality—a view in which the individual ego does not occupy the central position—perhaps death can be welcomed. And here we can identify the real issue behind the radically different positions outlined above. Are we able or willing to make the final "Copernican leap"? In other words, it seems to come down to the age-old question of an adequate cosmological model. History reveals that man has continually placed himself at the center, believing that reality somehow radiated out from him. The Ptolemaic view that the earth was the center of the universe was replaced by the initially upsetting concept that the sun occupied that position. Even that has been replaced with an Einsteinian model in which no privileged center is recognized. So we naturally cling to the ego as the starting point for reality. All directions begin at the location of our individual selves. It requires the greatest of all Copernican leaps to abandon that model of reality. But it can be done, and perhaps the truth is nearer when we do it. And where, after all, are integrity and dignity to be found? It is absurd to suppose that we must find our glory in error. If our individual egos are not the center of reality, if we ourselves must be understood as aspects of ultimate reality, then it would be a mark of maturity, of philosophical and psychological sophistication, to recognize that. We are not honored by whimpering and whining that we lack the perspective of the prophet, the poet, and the philosopher. We all have capacities beyond those achieved by us at the moment. If truth is worth pursuing, and if truth indicates that we are essentially more than our identifiable egos, then we must learn to let go of the ego. Perhaps death is to be welcomed as an entrance into reality itself, the very heart of truth.

This view is quite compatible with the feeling that death is a potential area for further knowledge. The exploration of death has helped us to gain a broader understanding of ourselves and the world into which we have been thrust. The study of death promises to reward us with a new perspective. There may be something noble in refusing to grant our approval to death. But there is also something sick about that. It is sick because it involves a contradiction which goes to the heart of mental and emotional illness. The contradiction is not a logical one but a psychological one. If we believe that death is something to be fought, despised, and rejected, then we have clearly failed to come to terms with reality. Death is real. In refusing to grant our approval we take on reality itself. We give support to the notion that we owe our allegiance to something other than ultimate reality, and what could that be? Presumably, only what is less than ultimate, or that which is unreal. Don Quixote, forever jousting with windmills which always emerge the victor, is understandable. But he is not really noble. He is tragic. He dreams the impossible dream, and therefore condemns himself to dreaming what is not, and can never be, real. The fact that by rejecting death we may see ourselves taking on the cosmos itself only makes our futility cosmic. If we are content to rage at the dying of the light, we succeed only in bringing to our efforts a proportion of frustration whose scope and magnitude are awesome. But such efforts can never be satisfying. Failure to come to terms with death is an admission of defeat, and emphasizing that failure is the equivalent of wallowing in our defeat. We simply cannot conquer death, and so a life based upon the notion that we can aims itself purposefully at failure. We cannot take on reality because there is nothing which could replace it. Reality cannot be exchanged for reality since that is a long-winded way of saying nothing. But reality can never be exchanged for anything else because by definition there is nothing else. Failure, then, to come to terms with reality must be frustrating. Further, it courts a sickness in the soul. Something about us is surely ultimately real. It is there that harmony and wholeness are to be found. Coming to terms with death is coming to terms with ourselves at our deepest level. Death is not to be feared, even if it means the annihilation of my ego. Whatever ultimate reality is, it is eternal since there is nothing greater which could destroy it. Ultimate reality can never become more than what it is, or it would not be ultimate. But neither can it become less, for then also it would no longer be ultimate. If we grant, as it seems we must, that *some*thing is ultimately real, then we are led to suppose that it is eternal. Further, either there is something ultimately real about us or there is not. If there is not, then our "reality" is but an illusion and therefore does not deserve our allegiance. If there is, then it is at that level that eternity will be a reality.

Carlos Castaneda, in his series of writings on the teachings of a Mexican Yaqui Indian, speaks of death as an adviser.[6] Living in the presence of our own death, learning from it, can serve to place our self-image in proper perspective. We can see ourselves against the incomparably larger form of eternity. We can see ourselves as we are. No intellectual discipline worthy of the name requires us to seek error. The assumption that it is truth, and not error, which deserves our allegiance is unproven. But we deny it at the risk of unacceptable physical and psychological chaos. Death has something to teach us, not only about the world, but, more important, about ourselves. Death *is* an adviser. It is therefore to be welcomed, if not joyfully, then at least thoughtfully. Socrates, who proclaimed death to be the goal of the true philosopher, proclaimed also that the first and great commandment of philosophy is to "know thyself."

174

There is a sense in which it is inappropriate to spend much effort in a book on death toward making the case that death is an adviser. That is really another way of saying that death is worth studying, and the existence of the book itself is, of course, predicated upon that assumption. But such a position brings rewards other than the mere accumulation of knowledge. As we come to know death we feel different about it. We may lose our fear of death. We may abandon the notion that death is an evil. We may even become excited about the metaphysical implications of death. But, having argued that death is to be confronted as an area of potential knowledge, we might be reminded by a thoughtful person that not all people are really so interested in the quest for knowledge. Before we consider how death ought to be confronted we should first ask whether or not everyone ought to confront death in the same way. Should we all cultivate the same attitude toward death? Is it somehow better for the individual, whether he be cabbage or king, to look at his death in some one, given way?

The immediate response to such a question might well be no. It is wrong to expect that there is a single approach to death which is somehow right for every individual. However we confront death we must not forget the variables involved. Death is not a single event, but many different events coming to many different individuals. We cannot ignore the significance of the particular situation in which death is encountered. Death is as individual as the ego that is taken. It comes from different directions to different people. Any suggestion that some single, given-in-advance attitude toward death is "the best" seems based upon the false assumption that there is such a thing as "the" death. Death is many things to many people, and these variables cannot be ignored in deciding how death is to be confronted. Those who are inclined to argue against the wisdom of promoting a universal approach to death can point to the

175

importance of such things as the physical and psychological health of one who is to die. Surely there is something more tragic about an individual who dies young, before he has had a chance to develop his capacities, than there is about a very elderly person who can look forward only to suffering. Can we expect that both should confront death in the same way? The source of death is also significant. In war, perhaps death is to be tolerated. In disease, perhaps death is to be feared. In old age, it may be that death is to be welcomed. We cannot seriously maintain, according to this line of reasoning, that death is to be faced in a single way without ignoring the many variables which attend every death, thereby making each death unique.

There is a strong point in this position. It is based upon the recognition that different situations require different responses, and it is difficult to take issue with that. But I am not convinced that we are dealing with different situations here. The process of dying is indeed unique in every case. No one who has had to deal with death can deny that. But the event of death itself is not so obviously unique. The metaphysics of death transcend any given situation. Death may come from varying sources to widely different people. It may be experienced in many different ways by those who are left behind. But the truth about death, whatever that may be, is one. Perhaps our analysis of death which sees it as the annihilation of the ego in favor of a more cosmic reality is wrong. The truth about death may lie elsewhere. But it does make sense to speak of "the truth" about death, even if we are not sure of the nature of that truth. The metaphysical truth about death is one and not many. This suggests that it is likely that there is some single view of death which is the best, in that it sees death for what it is.

Beyond that, we must remember that death has about it some very unique qualities. Death is inevitable. It is even more certain than taxes. Whatever we are, we were made for death. Further, we have seen that death is basic to an understanding of what we are. It tells us much about ourselves. It places us in a startling perspective. It shatters our narrow and parochial views about ourselves and the world, replacing them with a more cosmic orientation. Death is ultimate. It is our sure link with the heart of reality. We owe our existence, limited and petty as it may be, to the dynamic flux of ultimate reality. We share with all beings a relationship to the ground of being. The study of death is the search, not only for our ultimate destiny, but equally important for our ultimate origin as well. Somehow, for some reason, the universe has spit us out. But our subsequent existence is one of being continually drawn back to our source, which serves now as our destiny. The study of death is a consideration of the most important mysteries about us. Where did we come from? Where are we going? The pursuit of death is the study of both ends of the question of individual existence.

But if we are correct in believing that the ground of our reality is the ground of all reality, this indicates that our origins and destiny are shared by all other human beings. We have all been forged from the same hearth and will all return to the consuming fire. It is even likely that we share these things, not only with other human beings, but also with whatever exists in this world. The Einsteinian theories of relativity are not so complicated that we cannot gain from them a sense of the cosmic interrelatedness of all things. There is a relationship between me and all other existing things, and this relationship is more than a matter of words. I trace my lineage to the same God which grounds the reality of the earthworm, this page of print, and my wife. One whose interests are other than theological might prefer not to call the source of his being God, but the term is nevertheless appropriate. I do not know the nature of ultimate reality, although I do not mind making some guesses in this area. But I cannot escape acknowledging the reality of ultimate reality.

Whatever it is, it is there that I will find my own explanation.

What all this means is that it is likely that some attitudes toward death really are more "correct" than others. While granting the importance of the particular situation in which death is confronted, we must recognize also that death, whatever it involves, is the key to our common destiny. Furthermore, it is certainly the case that our attitude toward death is highly significant in determining the kind of persons we are. One of the most important contributions of the philosophical position known as existentialism is to be found in the significance attributed to the concept of alienation. The term has been used and abused until it has become almost trite. But life is in part a struggle against the feeling of alienation. We seek, whether we call it that or not, harmony, reconciliation, a sense of belonging. But how can this be achieved so long as we are ignorant of the deepest levels of self? It is, at bottom, an alienation from ourselves, or an ignorance about what we are, that troubles us. We are strangers in a strange land. Having no knowledge of where we have come from or where we are going, we cannot possibly know who we are. The words of Augustine become very appropriate: "Thou has made us for thyself, O God, and our hearts are restless till they rest in Thee." We cannot help seeking our source, anymore than water can avoid seeking its own level. But unlike water, we are aware that our desire is unfulfilled.

Life, then, can be understood as a tension between alienation and harmony, separation and reconciliation, plurality and union. Even if these terms are not used, the psychological truth remains. Existential absurdity is a function of the sense of alienation. We do not entirely feel as though we belong in this world. We are restless. And so we search for that in which we can find peace. And is it not interesting that this search generally goes in the direction of emphasizing our individuality? We cultivate the ego. We stress the distinction between the me and the not-me, and attempt to inflate the me against the not-me. But just a bit of reflection should reveal the futility in that effort. To the extent that we emphasize the individual ego, we make it impossible for a sense of harmony to occur. The ego exists only in opposition to that which it is not. It takes its form, its very definition, from the distinctions which separate it from all else. The ego, as we found in chapter 7, simply cannot exist without those qualities which distinguish it from the rest of the universe. But distinctions and separations are poor soil for the cultivation of harmony, reconciliation, and union. In our struggles to overcome the sense of alienation which produces a restlessness in us, we encourage the very qualities which ensure our failure. An exploration of the metaphysics of death begins, perhaps, to enlighten us at this very point. Our efforts are spent in the wrong direction. We are not unlike Augustine. We, like him, are driven from our deepest levels to seek peace. We cannot rest without it. We strive blindly to overcome alienation, only to find that our efforts serve to strengthen separation. Perhaps we must loosen our desperate grip on the ego. Perhaps death is the key.

This analysis of the human condition is not meant to picture the ego as an evil. It is, after all, only from the perspective of the ego that death can be studied. Knowledge *of* necessarily requires a distinction between the knowing subject and the object known. The ego is not to be despised or abused. It is not something to treat carelessly. The ego is our only vehicle to discovery. The potentialities which reside in the ego are profound. We can legitimately stand in awe of ourselves. If there is any meaning left to the word, we may even say that the ego is sacred. But the suggestion here is that it may not be ultimate. It would be difficult to argue that we owe our final allegiance to anything less than the ultimate. It is therefore possible to argue that we may not owe our final allegiance to ourselves.

179

POSTSCRIPT

Death is swallowed up in victory.
O death, where is thy victory?
O death, where is thy sting?

I never used those words in any funeral I ever conducted. This portion of Paul's First Letter to the Corinthians is often considered to be one of the most appropriate passages of scripture for a funeral service, but I consciously avoided it. It was simply not possible for me to stand beside a body dressed in various modes of artificiality, observe the intense grief of those whose lives had now to continue in the absence of a loved one, and pretend somehow that there is no sting in death. Death is always victorious, and the cadaver in the coffin taunts us with that fact. I have not changed my opinion. If I were conducting a funeral today, I would still not use that passage of scripture. The death of one we have known and loved brings to the living a sense of loss which can run about as deep as any emotion we are capable of experiencing. We can, and we must, learn to live with that loss. But we cannot forget it.

The sting of death is not easily overcome. I do not pretend that the considerations of death presented in this book will ease the anguish of one who must confront death, either in himself or in another. The pursuit of death as a metaphysical event sometimes bears little relation to death encountered as an existential event. But there is a healing balm in time. The passage of time, carrying the experience of the death of a loved one into the realms of memory, can allow us to gain a better perspective. It is then that an understanding of the nature of death can be psychologically useful, as well as intellectually interesting. There are metaphysical truths behind the existential event of death. We may find the moment of our confrontation with death no less severe for having wrestled with death at the level of metaphysics. But we will not carry that moment with us forever. The memory of death and the mysteries of death—these will remain. Our curiosity about death is not idle. Nor is it perverted. Death is frightening, in part, because it is unknown. And this fear does not ease with the passage of time. It can be countered only by knowledge. Our fears of death will surely lessen with an increase in our understanding of what death is and how we are threaded with it into the fabric of reality. The grief felt in the moments following the death of a friend is not primarily due to our ignorance about death. It is the sense of irreversible loss which brings us pain. It is difficult to see how metaphysics can help us here. But later, when that pain subsides, as it must, there remains an awesome ignorance which will continue to weigh upon us. Whatever help may be found in this book will have to be here.

Paul also spoke of leaving undone things which ought to have been done, and some may feel that this observation is quite appropriate to this book. There are countless areas within the general topic of death that have not been explored. Because of the philosophical orientation taken in this book, there has been no attempt to explore death through the distinctions of history and culture. We have not provided any information on the variations of funeral customs and the beliefs behind them, nor have we even analyzed our own customs in this area. We have not dealt in depth with the psychological aspects of death. But these are areas beyond the scope of this book.

It can be pointed out, however, that we have also ignored many philosophically interesting issues in death. There has been no extensive analysis of the more traditional views. We have not examined any of the traditional arguments for or against immortality. The fairly extensive treatment of death in the existentialist school of thought has been largely ignored. The very fascinating and useful insights of linguistic analysis in this area have also been avoided. We may be faulted for not dealing adequately with the very serious problem of personal identity which has been emphasized by analytic philosophers in their considerations of immortality. There are, of course, the various moral issues raised in a study of death. We have not even suggested an adequate response to the question of suicide, which Albert Camus said was the *only* truly serious philosophical problem. Further, philosophy certainly has an obligation to direct its attention to the increasingly important question of euthanasia, or mercy-killing. We must come to terms with the claim that an individual has the right to choose death.

But it has not been our intention to write an encyclopedia of death. Any work which can fit between two covers must necessarily have its limits. The metaphysics of death is an area not widely treated. There are data available today which may be significant in helping us to understand death at that level. There is a need for speculation on the basis of contemporary information, and this book has served as an outlet for one such attempt.

But all this only masks the real purpose of the book. It has been my intention to give the reader a sense of the excitement of exploration in uncharted realms. We, like the first explorers of the great caves, do not have the advantages of reliable maps. We cannot rely on any existing illumination, and so we must grope our way forward into the dark recesses of the unknown. And if occasionally we leave smudge marks because our torches are primitive and inadequate, perhaps later adventurers with better equipment will forgive us. They will know what we do not.

They will have charts and superior lighting. Their exploration will be sure and safe. But however many tourists subsequently visit the metaphysical caves of death, their greater illumination will reveal something they have missed and can never know—our smudge marks, which proclaim that we were there first.

NOTES

2. Toward a Definition of Death

1. This is suggested in an article by Geoffrey Gorer, "The Pornography of Death," *Encounter*, October, 1955, pp. 46-52.
2. J. J. Bruhier-d'Ablaincourt, *Mémoire sur la nécessité d'un réglement général au sujet des enterrements et des embauments, et projet de réglement*, Paris, 1746. These and other cases are cited in A. K. Mant's essay, "The Medical Definition of Death," in Arnold Toynbee, *et al.*, *Man's Concern with Death* (New York: McGraw-Hill, 1968), pp. 12 ff.
3. Ethics in Medical Progress, Ciba Foundation Symposium, Churchill, London, 1966, p. 69. Cited in *Man's Concern with Death*, p. 22.
4. Quoted in Marya Mannes, *Last Rights* (New York: William Morrow, 1974), p. 57.
5. H. Beecher, *The New York Times*, December 10, 1967. Cited in *Man's Concern with Death*, p. 23.
6. This position is taken by R. S. Morison in his essay, "Death: Process or Event?" *Science*, August, 1971, pp. 694-98. L. R. Kass responds to this in the same issue in "Death as an Event: A commentary on Robert Morison," pp. 575-85.
7. Victor D. Solow won a Reader's Digest "First Person" award with an article by this title, printed in *Reader's Digest*, October, 1974, pp. 178-82.

3. The Soul

1. Plato, *Phaedo*, in Lane Cooper, trans., *Plato on the Trial and Death of Socrates* (Ithaca, N.Y.: Cornell University Press, 1967), p. 178.
2. A Brief critical evaluation of these theories is presented by Milič Čapek in his book, *The Philosophical Impact of Contemporary Physics* (New York: Van Nostrand, 1961), pp. 282 ff.
3. *Ibid.*, p. 306.
4. A. D. Allen, "Does Matter Exist?" *Intellectual Digest*, June, 1974, p. 60.

4. Death as a Uniquely Human Event

1. Albert Camus, *The Myth of Sisyphus and Other Essays* (New York: Vintage Books, 1955), p. 3.

2. T. V. Smith, ed., *Philosophers Speak for Themselves: From Thales to Plato* (Chicago: University of Chicago Press, 1956), p. 12.
3. J. White, ed., *The Highest State of Consciousness* (Anchor Books; Garden City, N.Y.: Doubleday, 1972), p. xv.
4. *Ibid.,* p. xvi.

6. Philosophy, Science, and Death

1. C. G. Jung, "Psychological Commentary," in W. Y. Evans-Wentz, *The Tibetan Book of the Dead* (London: Oxford University Press, 1963), pp. xli ff.
2. Arthur Koestler, *The Roots of Coincidence* (New York: Vintage Books, 1972), p. 11.
3. *Ibid.,* p. 32
4. A. E. Taylor, *The Christian Hope of Immortality* (London: The Centenary Press, 1938), pp. 19-20.
5. J. Cass, "What It's Like to Die," *Today, The Philadelphia Inquirer,* November 3, 1974, p. 29.
6. (New York: Macmillan, 1969.)
7. J. Y. Dayananda, "The Death of Ivan Ilych: A Psychological Study on Death and Dying," *Literature and Psychology,* Vol. XXII, No. 4, 1972.
8. *The Roots of Coincidence,* p 64.
9. For a further exploration of this suggestion the reader is encouraged to consider A. A. Cochran's essay, "Mind, Matter, and Quanta, " in *Main Currents,* March-April, 1966, pp. 79-88.
10. J. Avorn, "Beyond Dying," *Harper's* magazine, March, 1973, p. 62.
11. W. Pahnke, "The Psychedelic Mystical Experience in the Human Encounter with Death," *Harvard Theological Review,* January, 1969, p. 6.
12. H. K. Beecher, "Response to the Ingersoll Lecture by a Physician," *Harvard Theological Review,* January, 1969, p. 23.
13. W. G. Roll, "Psychical Research in Relation to Higher States of Consciousness," in White, *The Highest State of Consciousness,* p. 465.

7. Ego Death

1. David Hume, "Personal Identity," Sec. VI, printed in A. J. Ayer and R. Winch, eds., *British Empirical Philosophers* (New York: Simon & Schuster, 1968), p. 483.

8. Immortality

1. Melissus, "The Nature of Reality," printed in G. L. Abernethy and T. Langford, eds., *History of Philosophy* (Belmont, Cal.: Dickenson Publishing Company, 1965), p. 23

2. Antony Flew, "Death," in Flew and A. MacIntyre, *New Essays in Philosophical Theology* (New York: Macmillan, 1964), p. 267.
3. Quoted in William James, *The Varieties of Religious Experience* (New York: University Books, 1963), p. 399.

9. Confronting Death

1. e. e. cummings, "dying is fine but Death" XAIPE, 1950, in *Poems 1923*–54 (New York: Harcourt Brace Jovanovich), p. 451.
2. Dylan Thomas, "Do not go gentle into that good night," *The Collected Poems of Dylan Thomas* (New York: New Directions, 1952), p. 128.
3. Edna St. Vincent Millay, "Dirge Without Music," from *Collected Poems* (New York: Harper, 1928, 1955).
4. Plato, *Phaedo,* in *The Republic and Other Works,* B. Jowett, trans. (Dolphin Books; Garden City, N.Y.: Doubleday, 1960), p. 495.
5. Kahlil Gibran, *The Prophet* (New York: Alfred A. Knopf, 1951), pp. 80-81.
6. *Journey to Ixtlan* (New York: Simon & Schuster, 1972), pp. 46 ff.

INDEX

Index of Scripture References

Index of Subjects